ON CHRISTOPHER STREET: TRANSGENDER STORIES

On CHRIS STREET: GENDER PHOTOG MARK SE

TOPHER

TRANS-

STORIES

RAPHS *by*

LIGER

RIZZOLI
NEW YORK

New York · Paris · London · Milan

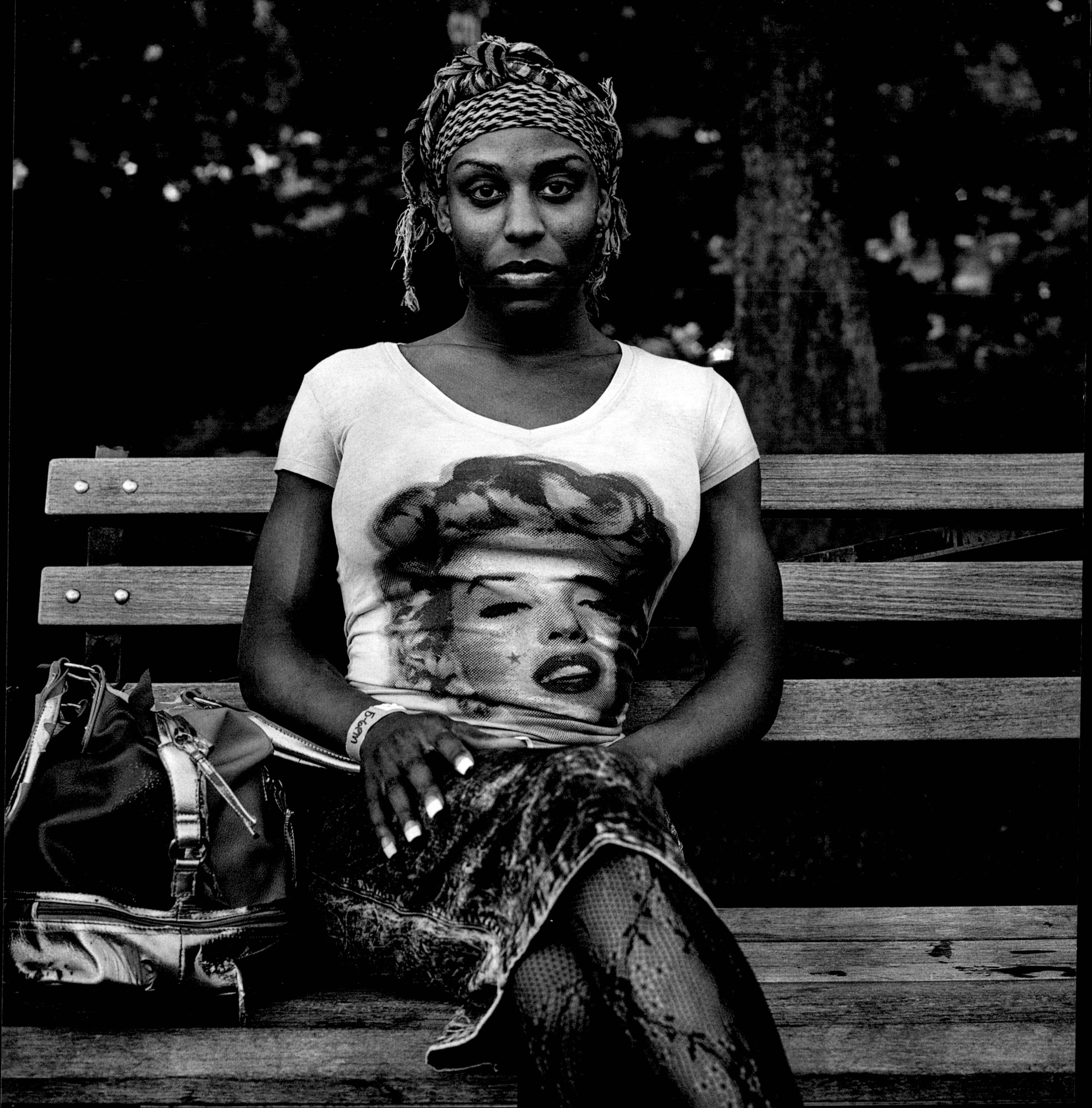

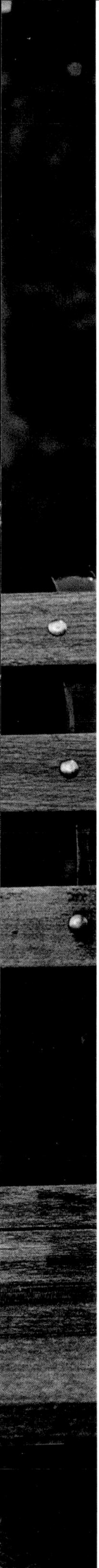

I've always been intrigued by the life and theatre of Christopher Street. I've noticed the photographic possibility out of the corner of my eye for the past couple of decades—an Ellis Island for freedom of expression and gender identity. More recently, I've noticed it vanishing. My interest in photo documentary led to the building of a series of portraits, which led to three summers of shooting. At first I didn't even realize I was shooting trans stories, just stories of people who found their way to Christopher Street. As I began to talk about this project, I realize that everybody has a trans story, that being trans is something that affects all of us.

—MARK SELIGER, 2016

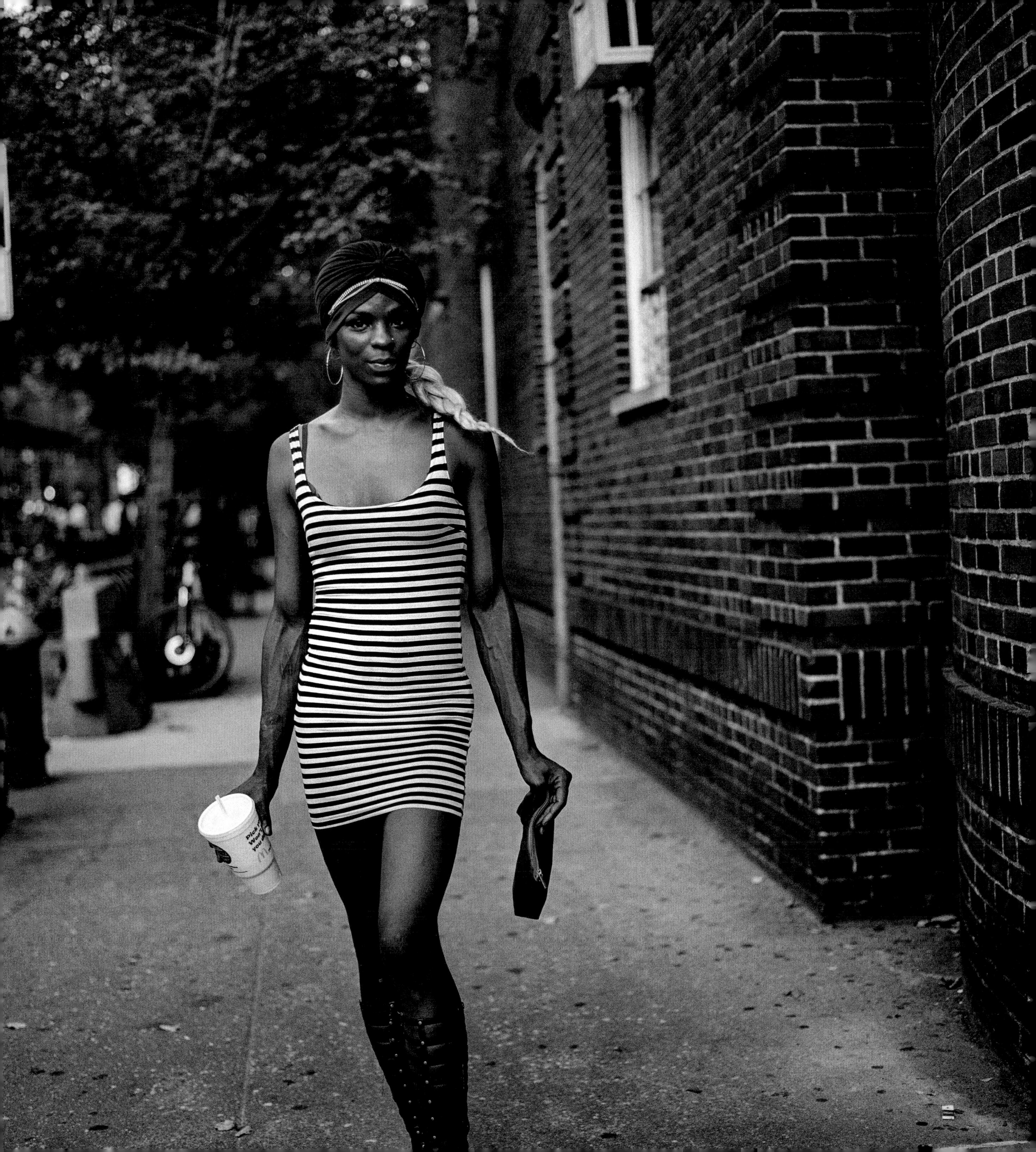

On Christopher Street

foreword by Janet Mock

THE FIRST IMAGE that left an indelible impression on me was a film still of Venus Xtravaganza, a twenty-something trans woman, standing on the Christopher Street Pier in New York City. I can recall it from memory: The sun setting over the Hudson River turned the sky into streams of navy, yellow, and magenta. Her voluminous blond hair hovered over her lanky body, adorned with a lime-green vest and chunky bangles. She positioned her cigarette with grace between her fingers as if she were in an ad. A silver boom box idly competed with her in the frame.

Venus appeared attractive yet approachable, tough yet vulnerable, and unapologetically femme. She resembled the girls I grew up with in Honolulu, the ones who beat their faces and snatched their curves every night to walk Merchant Street and Kuhio Avenue, the most traveled trails for Oahu's trans women.

I was fifteen, just embarking on becoming my own woman, when I locked eyes on Venus in that still from *Paris Is Burning,* the 1990 documentary by Jennie Livingston that followed black and Latina trans women, drag queens, and gay youth in New York City's ball culture. It was the first time I saw a girl like myself centered in a film that captured a mainstream audience's attention. It felt like the first time a young trans woman publicly spoke about the world as she knew it. Venus talks about her dreams of matrimony and domesticity, the tough realities of sex work, the fear of AIDS, and the threat of violence that overwhelmingly looms over young, low-income trans women, especially those of color. These were truths I knew too well as a girl who hustled to take care of myself in poverty-stricken neighborhoods that had limited resources to care for me.

Despite the hardships, Venus had the resourceful and affirming embrace of her chosen family—other trans, gay, and gender-nonconforming people she found through the ballroom. She talked lovingly about Hector Xtravaganza, the founding father of the House of Xtravaganza ("The first gay man I ever met") who threw her a fifteenth birthday party in the Village. Her first time in the Village turned out to be fateful.

"I met a lot of drag queens and transvestites that I didn't believe were because they were so beautiful," she said, "and that kind of sunk into my head, and I guess that's why it kind of made me want to do it more."

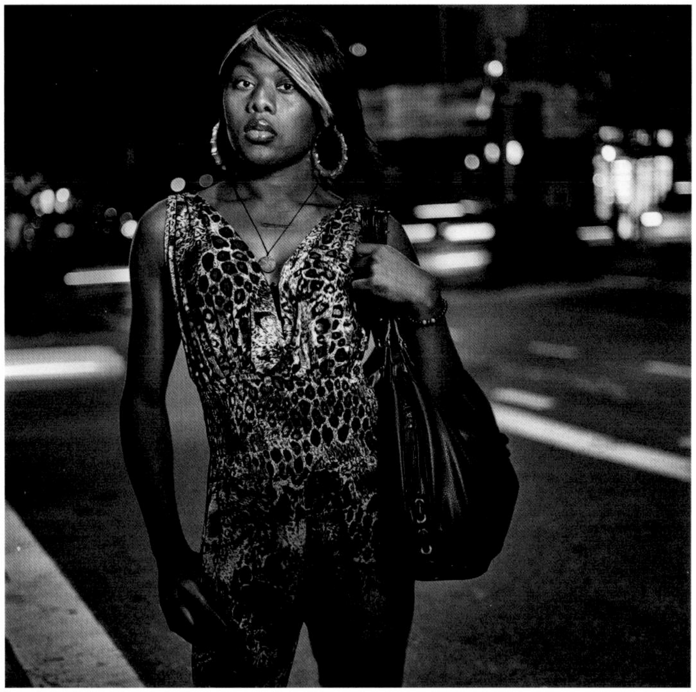

It was in the Village, on Christopher Street and the piers, where generations of young trans and queer people first shared lived space with others like them. This place provided mirrors to those who rarely saw reflections of themselves. On Christopher Street there are all kinds of sexual orientations and gender identities, endless possibilities of potential selves: transgender, transsexual, non-binary, genderqueer, femme, butch, cross-dresser, drag kings, drag queens, and many other identities that shift, adapt and challenge our understanding of gender.

Christopher Street is a beacon for those who are questioning, seeking, and exploring self. A bright flame signaling safety and freedom from oppression.

Many who hold Christopher Street close are captured on its pavements by Mark Seliger. Each shares the significance of this one American street: Jevon considers Christopher Street "my beginning"; Leiomy called it "a place where you didn't have to be looking behind your back"; and Egypt said it "became my home. I lived on the piers for years because I had nowhere to go."

Egypt is not alone. Homeless LGBTQ youth represent 40 percent of the nation's young people living on the streets. Rejected by unaccepting families, pushed out of hostile schools and foster care systems, and with limited access to welcoming and affirming shelters or means to secure employment, the streets become home for many who remain susceptible to state harassment and violence, criminalization, HIV/AIDS, assault, and drug abuse.

For most Americans, the street is a passageway to one's destination. But for displaced trans, queer, and gender-nonconforming people seeking community and guidance—the street is the destination. The street teaches you about living your truth, about accessing vital healthcare, about navigating shelter systems, about remaining safe in underground economies. It's a vital resource with tools the outside world doesn't have access to. Your people on Christopher Street become life-changing guides.

Historically, Christopher Street and the pier have been havens for LGBTQ people. In the late 1950s, queer folk and trans people began gathering and cruising in the area, which was all but abandoned with the decline of the shipping industry. The pier, Christopher Street, and the Village soon became the city's most visible and public space for sexual freedom and gender nonconformity.

As visibility of LGBTQ people increased, city officials tried to suppress and control queer and trans people's expressions, identities, and sexualities. People of the same sex were banned from dancing with each other. Bars were prohibited from serving alcohol to gay people. Sumptuary laws enforced the gender binary by outlawing cross-dressing or gender nonconformity by requiring people to wear at least three items of clothing that correlated with their documented assigned sex. Trans and queer people were living under a heavily policed state for years before screaming "No more!"

On June 27, 1969, police raided Stonewall Inn, a popular gay bar on Christopher Street. Inhabitants of the hot spot others on the street, including homeless people, drag queens, street youth, queer people of color, and trans folk like Sylvia Rivera and Marsha P. Johnson, resisted and fought back. Over the following days, thousands protested the police action. According to many accounts, the rebellion was started by those who had nothing—no assets, no property, no familial obligations. All they had was their bodies and their lives, which they put on the front line for liberation. They fought on these streets because the streets belonged to them.

Today, Christopher Street is heralded as the birthplace of the modern LGBTQ rights movement. Tourists stop by for a photo opp at Stonewall Inn; the intersction at Christopher and Hudson Streets has been renamed "Sylvia Rivera Way," after the pioneering trans activist; and the LGBTQ pride parade ends its procession on Christopher Street,

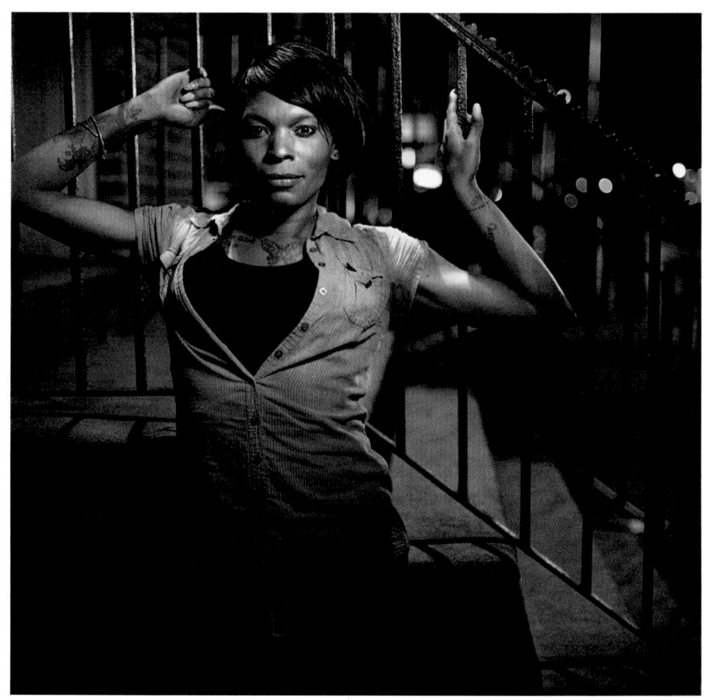

On Christopher Street there are all kinds of sexual orientations and gender identities, endless possibilities of potential selves: transgender, transsexual, non-binary, genderqueer, femme, butch, cross-dresser, drag kings, drag queens, and many other identities that shift, adapt and challenge our understanding of gender.

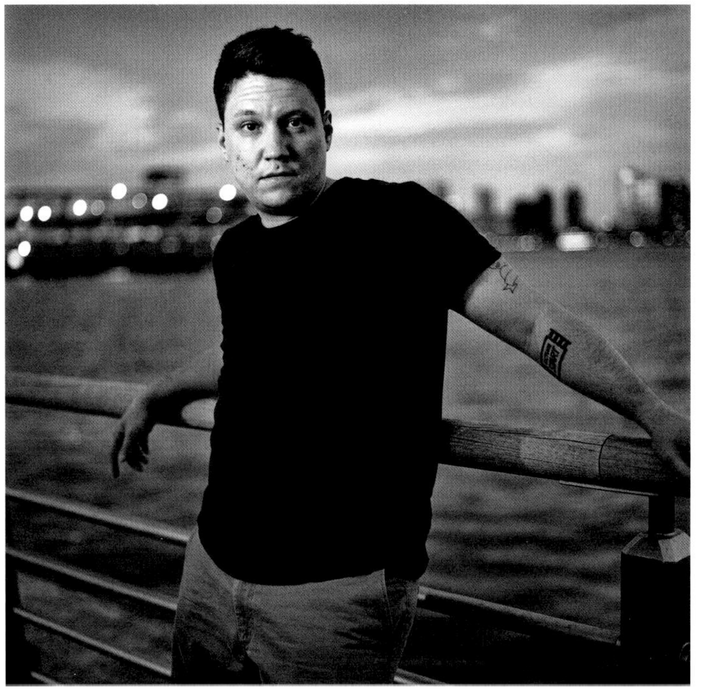

where the revolution began. The Stonewall Inn, Christopher Park located across the street, and the surrounding neighborhood are listed on the New York State Register of Historic Places.

Nearly fifty years have passed since the rebellion, but the fight continues for LGBTQ people, particularly those from low-income and people-of-color communities. The Christopher Street of today has replaced gay dives, cruising, and fetish shops with children's furniture stores, coffee shops, and luxury clothing boutiques, all catering to new affluent residents who have invested in the skyrocketing real estate market.

As Christopher Street, the piers, and the Village succumb to gentrification, the attitude toward young and low-income people who have frequented the area for generations has changed. Class and race tensions remain high in the neighborhood, with common complaints about noise, litter, and loitering. To curb this problem, police presence in the area has increased, making it appear safer for those with resources and unwelcoming for those without. There is also a 1 a.m. curfew at the piers, an area that previously didn't have such restrictions, further limiting access to a safe space for those who cannot afford rent in the luxury high-rises that now line the waterfront.

Organizations like FIERCE, which builds leadership of LGBTQ youth of color, The Door, which provides comprehensive youth services, and the Audre Lorde Project's Trans Justice, which organizes the annual Trans Day of Action, are adamant about demanding justice and increasing the presence of LGBTQ people in public spaces that have long been their own.

I have attended Trans Day of Action since 2011 and have been filled with pride while chanting "Whose streets? Our streets!" alongside hundreds of demonstrators. Marching on the streets of the Village, you're confronted by the pavement's refusal to succumb to Manhattan's rectangular grid geography. The jagged, unpredictable street patterns of Christopher and its surrounding streets are a visual metaphor of the plight of trans and queer people. There is no straight way to liberation.

Images have the power to strike us, teach us, and reflect us. It is the image that achieves all three that truly leaves us. That image of Venus on the Christopher Street Pier still haunts me.

The bold, blond, and blunt documentary film subject didn't survive to see herself on the big screen. She was found strangled to death under a hotel bed. She was just twenty-three. I wish I could say that Venus's tragic end is rare for my sisters, but low-income trans women, especially those of color, face an epidemic of violence that occurs at intersections of racism, sexism, and anti-trans bias.

Venus's last words in *Paris Is Burning* are "I'm hungry." Simply, it is a call for food, but I hear a resounding call for comfort, for love, for community, for home—a communal call from trans people on Christopher Street as well as those spanning across our country, from Honolulu's Merchant Street and Chicago's Halstead Street to San Francisco's Tenderloin and beyond.

Open spaces—spaces where you don't have to spend money but can be with your people—are necessary. We exist at a time when trans people are being seen and heard in unprecedented ways yet are being demonized by polarizing political rhetoric aiming to push the most vulnerable out of public spaces, from bathrooms and schools to healthcare and employment.

We must be vigilant about protecting public space from the interest of systems looking to displace our most marginalized neighbors. These forthcoming portraits of trans people on Christopher Street remind us of our need for sanctuary, for a space to call our own. Their presence challenges us to redefine home, community, and ownership. Their presence challenges us to stop and reflect. No longer will we remain idle and pass by them in fear and prejudice. We will stand with them, recognize them, and see them. These are our streets, and these are our people.

"She's a trans woman and I'm a trans man, so it actually makes us completely normal. I'm a man and she's a woman, and that's just as simple as it is."

—JAMEL YOUNG

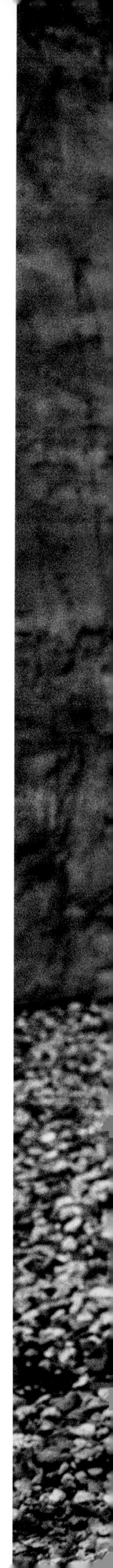

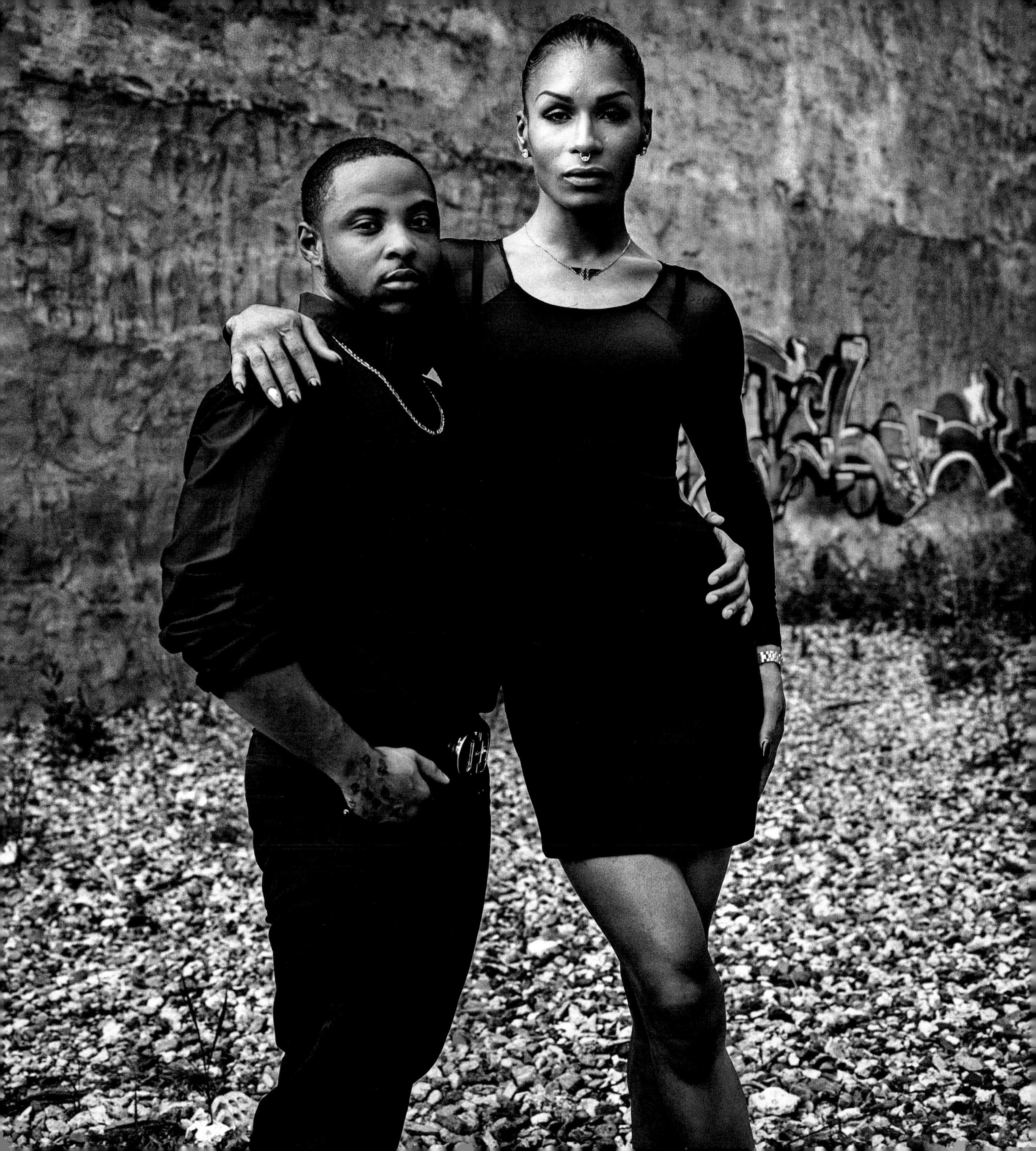

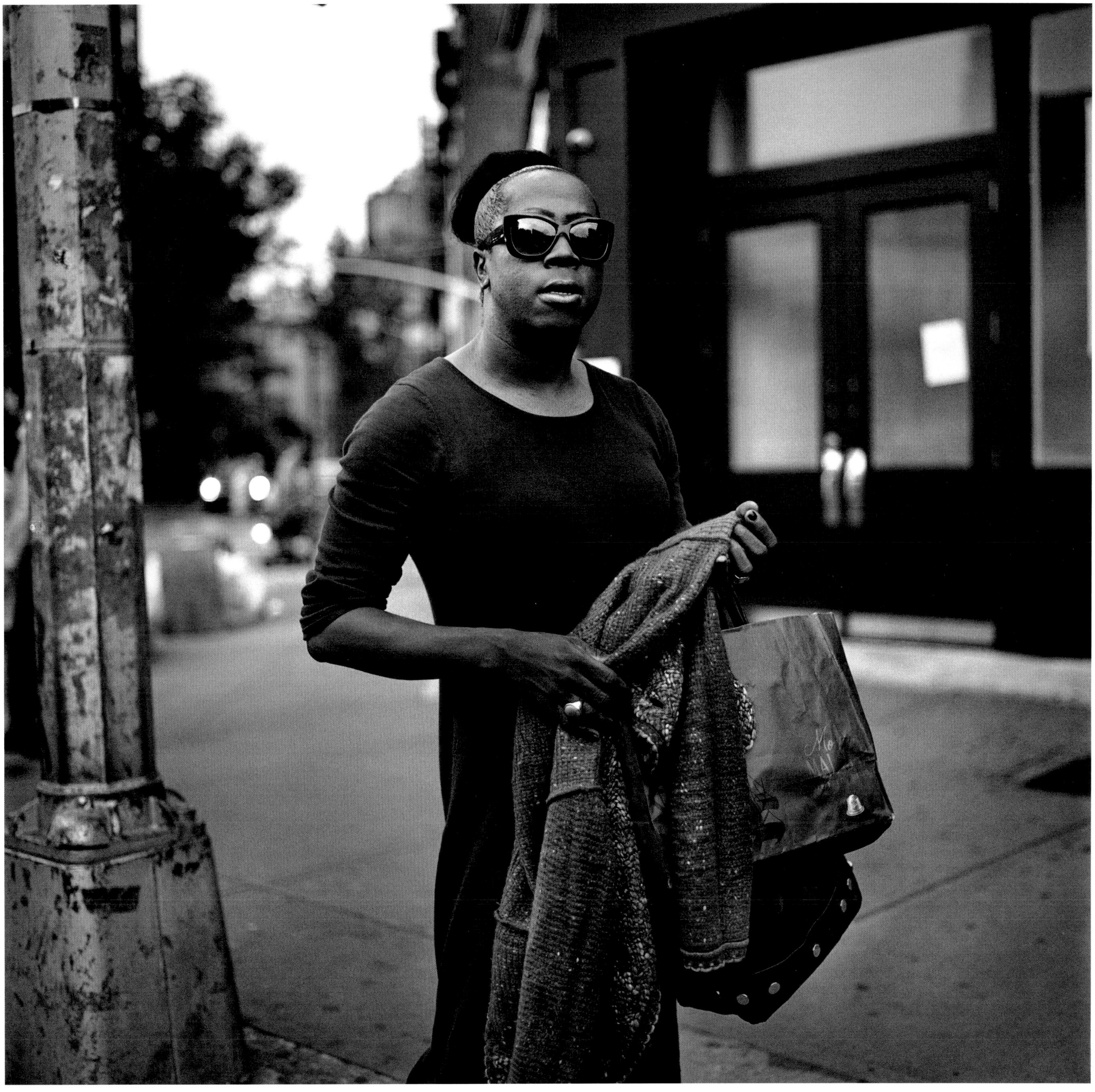

I WAS BORN IN LITTLE ROCK, Arkansas, and raised in Memphis, Tennessee. Growing up in Little Rock, well, I was very different from the other kids. I was a very effeminate child. And I was very artistic as well. I was very musically inclined; I sang in the church and later I started singing onstage, in plays and on Broadway.

My first realization that I was in the wrong body was when my mother told me I was using the restroom incorrectly. That was my first awakening that I was not who I thought I was.

But I still did not come to terms with it until I was thirteen or fourteen. I started to transition at a very young age—you know, I would put a towel on my head and pretend it was long hair and I would prance around as though everything were very glamorous.

From very early on, I felt trapped. I was actually incarcerated for ten years, and I can't say that I have necessarily ever really felt freedom. Because I was in prison, I couldn't transition and I felt caged. Being a trans woman and being incarcerated in a male's institution was surreal. The guys knew I didn't belong there, I knew I didn't belong there, and the staff knew I didn't belong there. They didn't have a proper place for me, so I was tossed around a lot within the Department of Corrections. And there was a lot of sexual activity going on, and the officers would use tricks and tactics and threats in order to obtain sex.

Transitioning back into society after my release from prison was very difficult. I had been off the hormones I'd been on since I was fourteen, and the guards wanted to give me a little smack in the face after I was released, so they made me a new ID and put my old name on it, misgendering me. So when I went out to the bus terminal or I was trying to get food stamps or something, it was very difficult just to get the basic necessities because I had to go through this long drawn-out story to explain who I was.

I always wanted to be the next Whitney. That was my dream. And my dreams have come true. After one door opened, they all kind of bust open.

I was very close with my mother until she found out I was transgender. And then our relationship became a little estranged, and I wound up running away at the age of fourteen. I was in foster care and, later, a temporary ward of the state, and at seventeen I was emancipated and I didn't look back.

—ShaGasyia Diamond

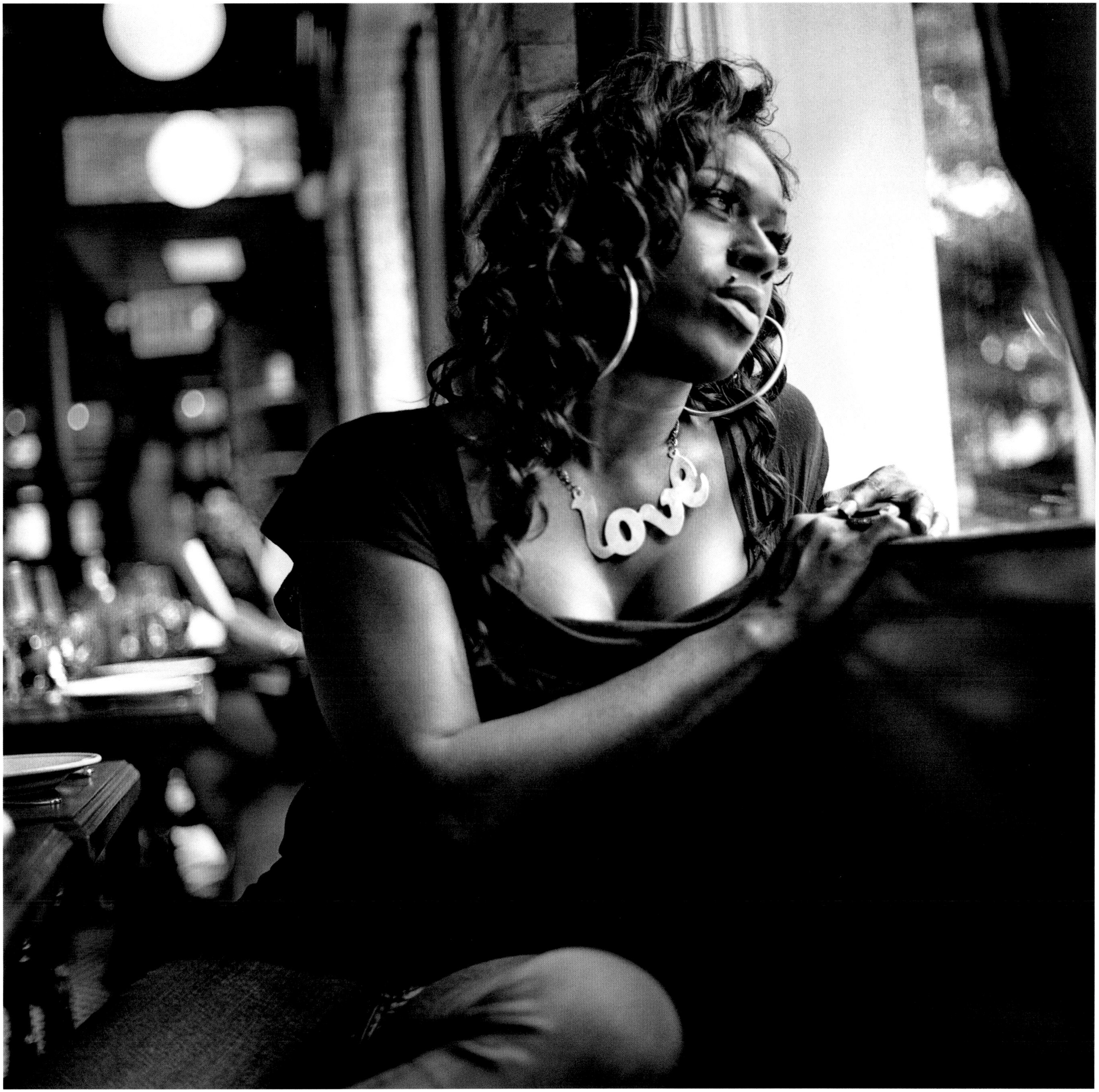
love

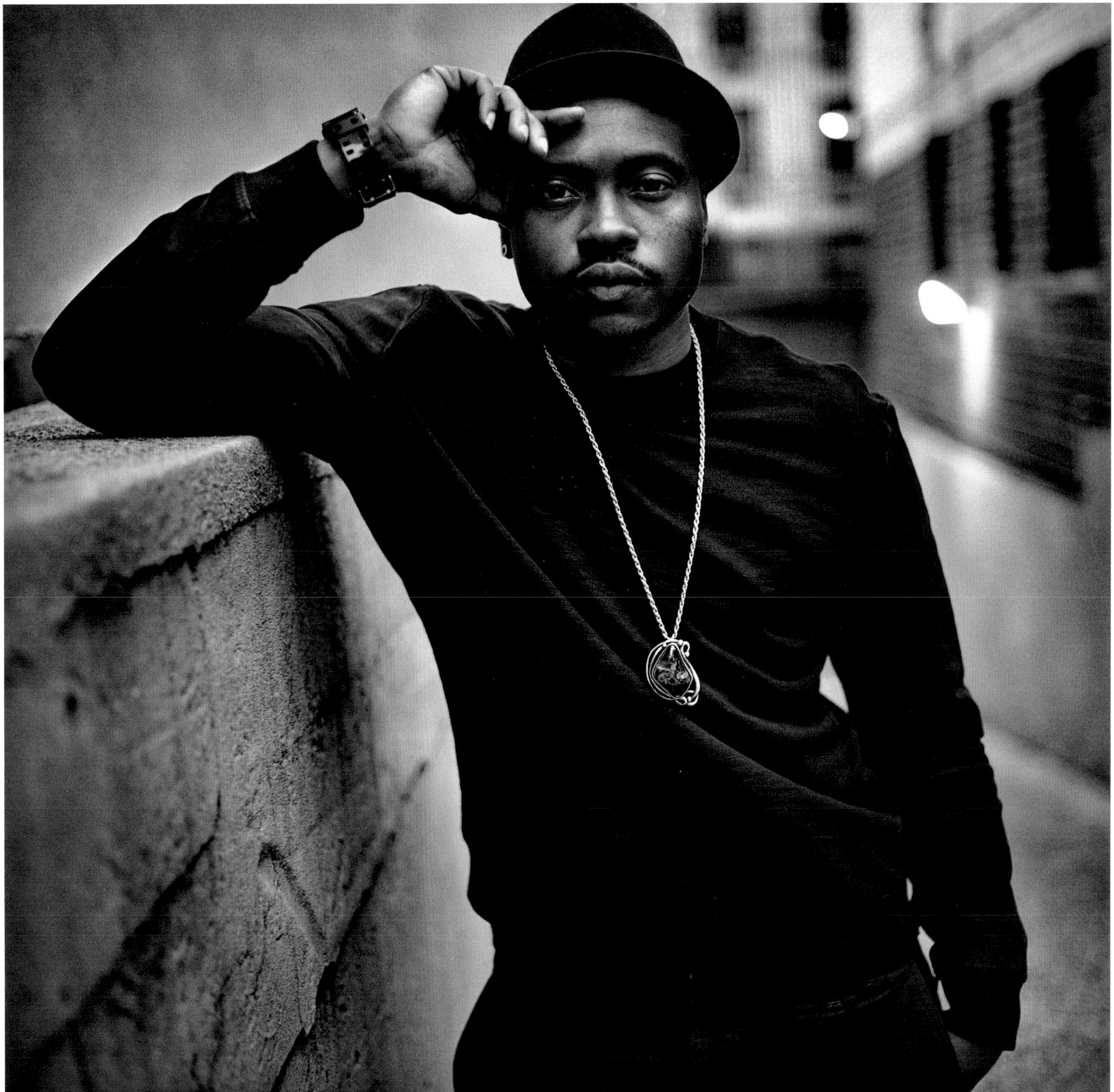

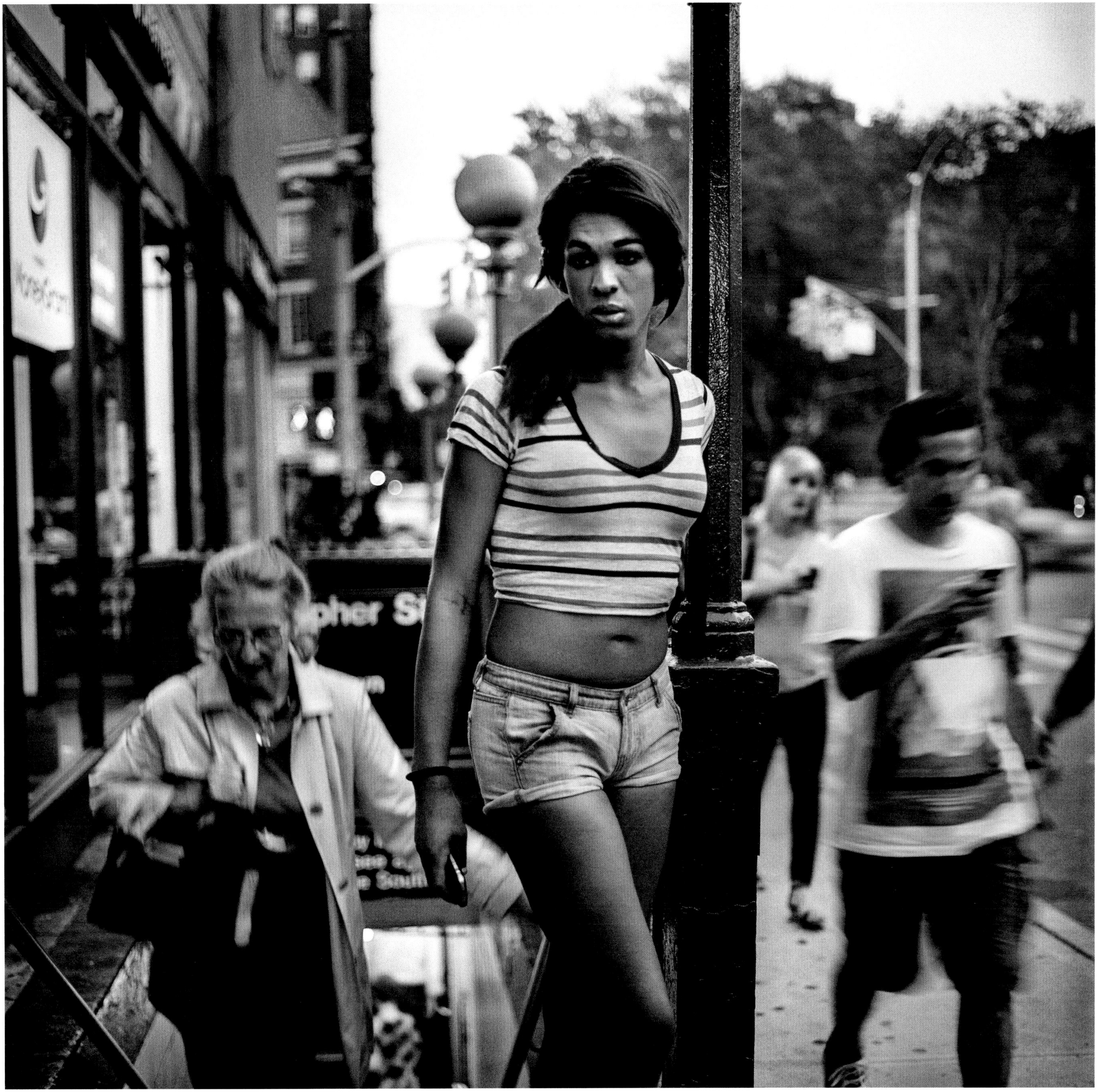

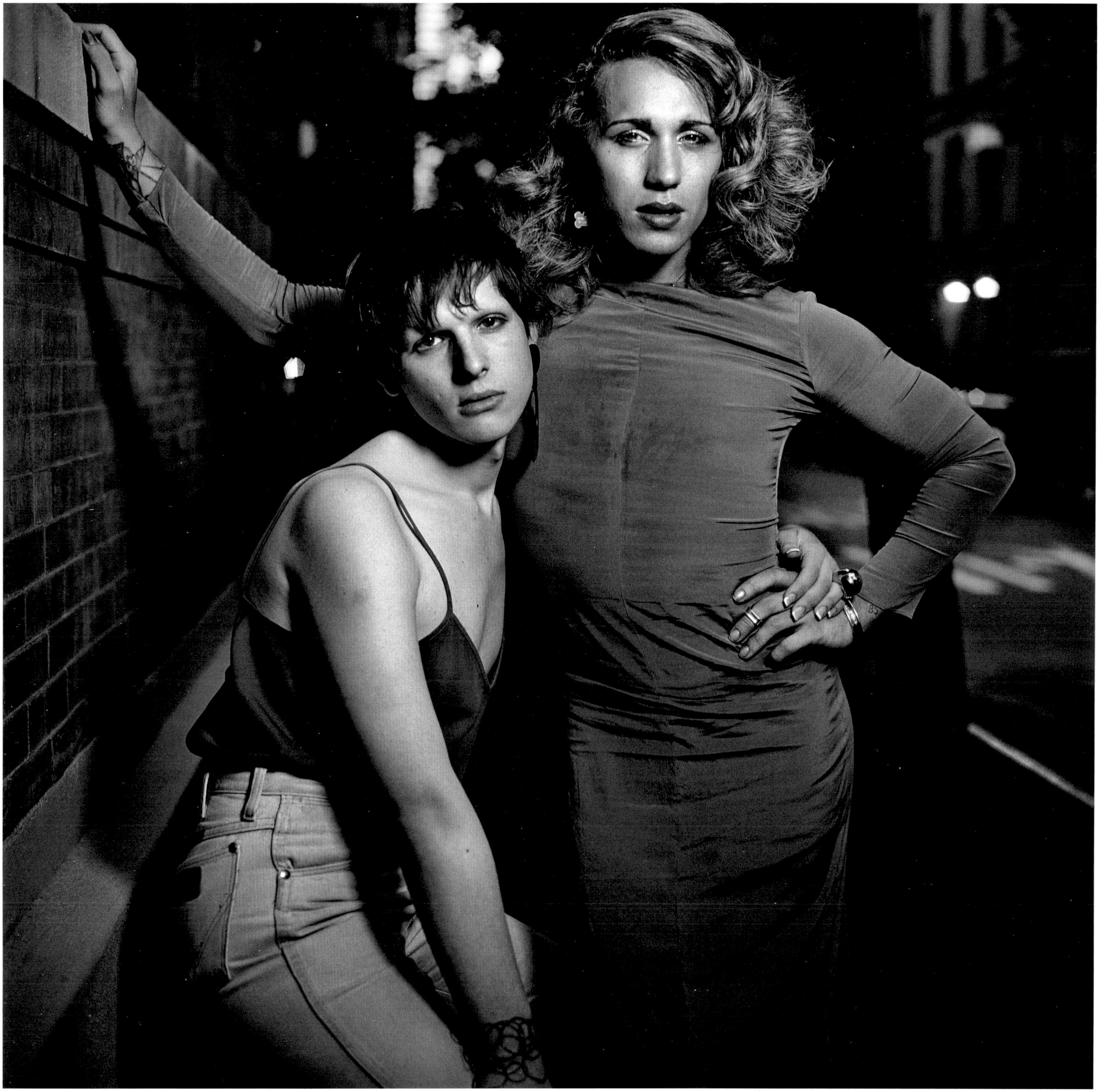

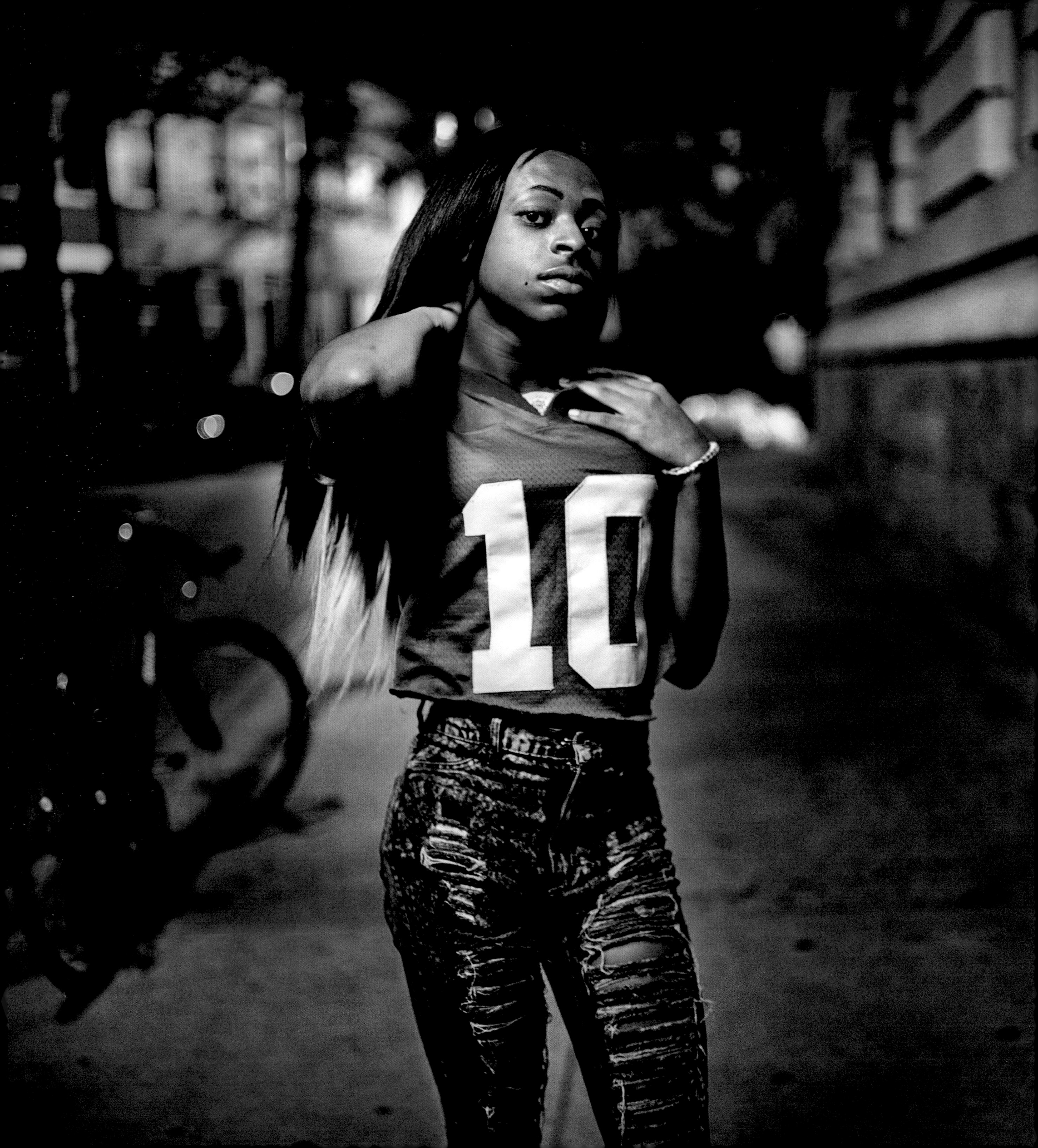
10

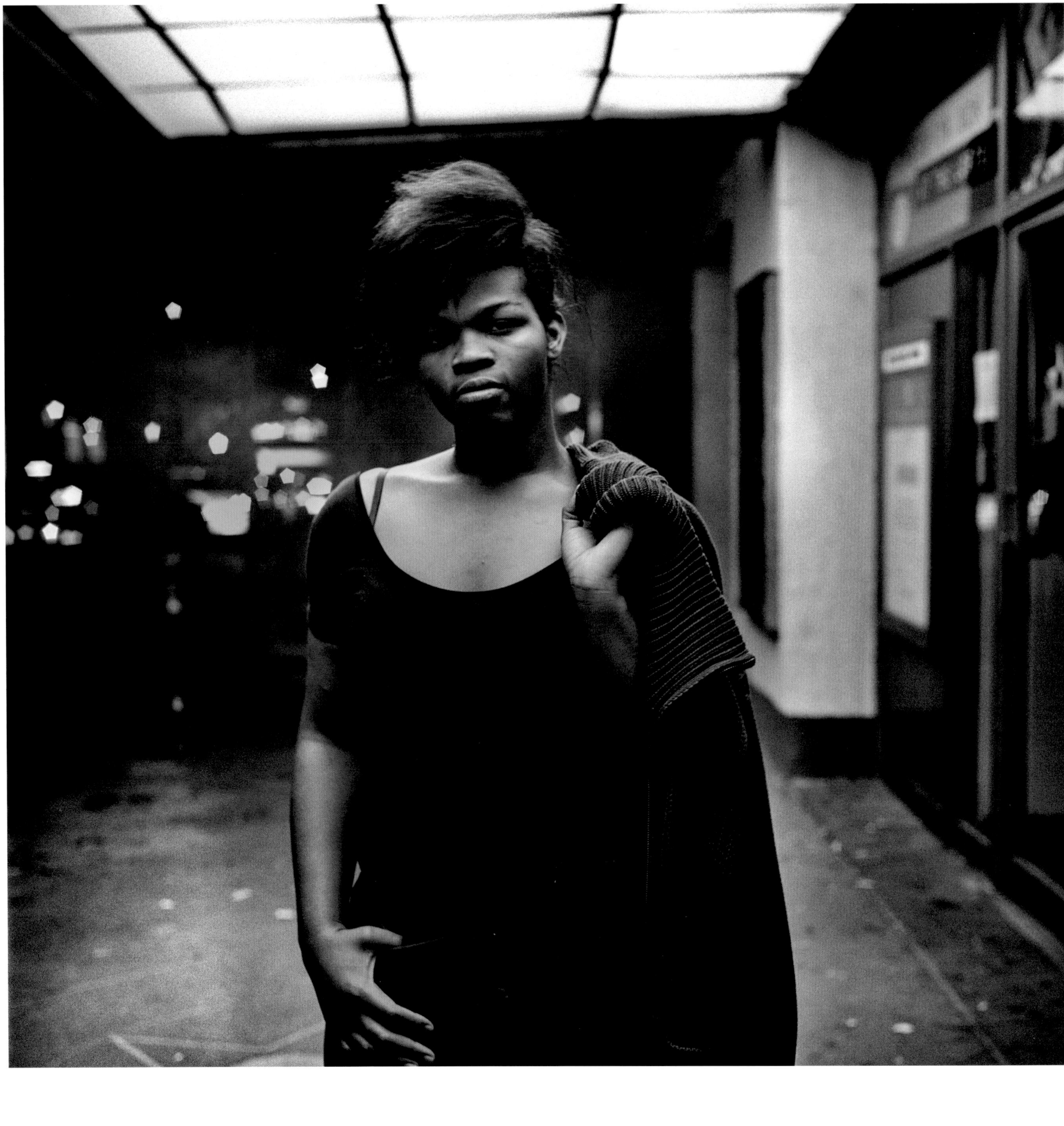

KEYANNA BANGER

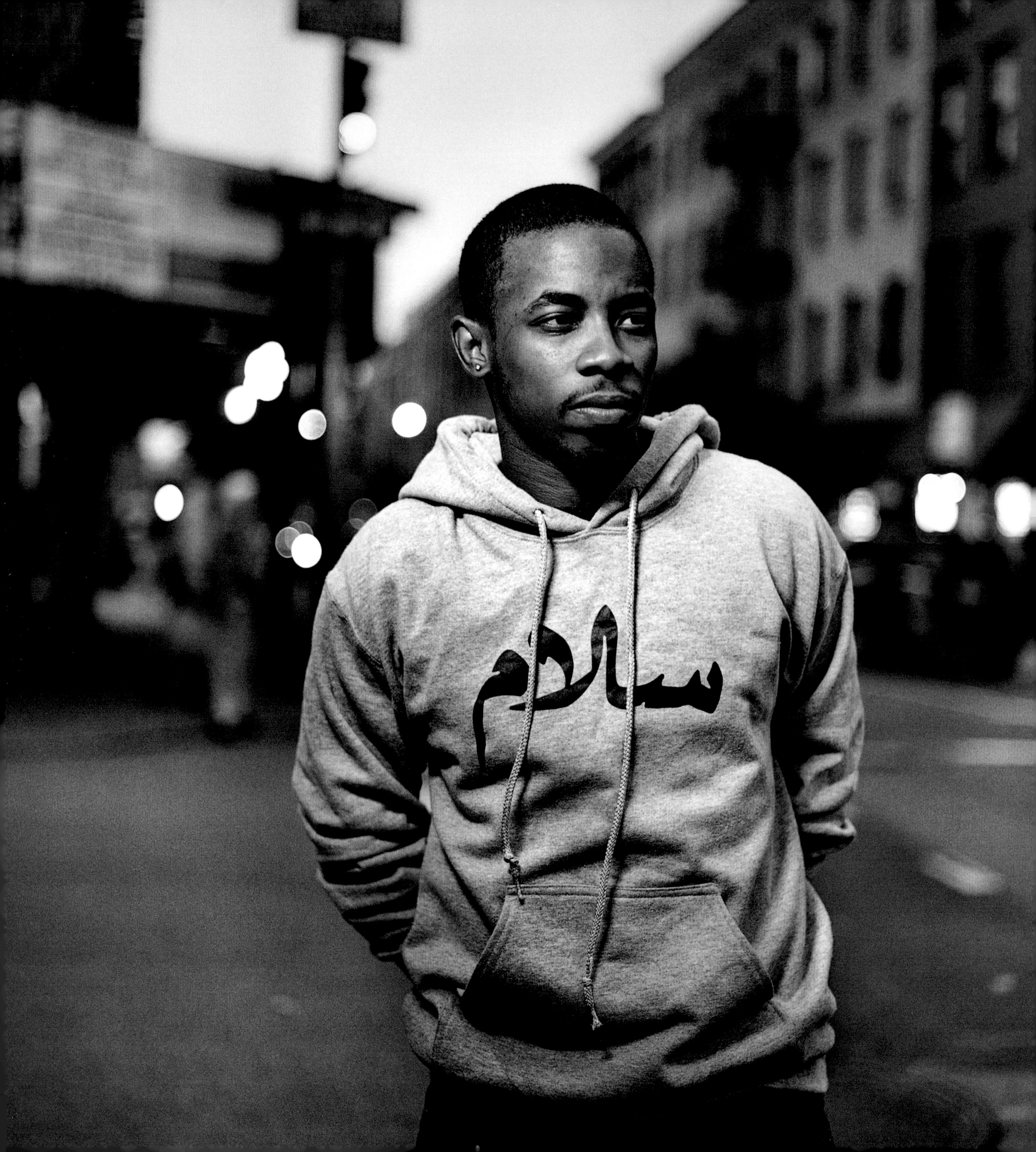
سلام

I WAS FOUR when I told my mother and father I was a boy. Parents don't believe that their kids at that age really know what they're going through; they think everything is a phase. But I was four years old and I was uncomfortable with the body that I was born in. This was well before you have sexual hormones, so it had nothing to do with sexual orientation and everything to do with gender identity. Everything I identified with was the opposite of the sex I was assigned at birth. I played with "boy" toys, I played at sports; I never played with Barbies or dressed in anything feminine. My parents were young, and they actually let me pick out my own clothes and thought I was just being a tomboy.

When I walked through those clinic doors to start the hormone process at age nineteen, I was totally prepared because I had been identified with my gender since I was four. Being on hormones or having certain surgeries is not what makes you transgender. Your gender is internal. Everyone is different. My preference for my transition was to start hormone therapy and have surgery. I'm a determined individual. I found a clinic in the Bronx and initiated the first steps: pre-interview, pre-therapy. They need to determine if you are qualified to transition with the government paperwork in the state of New York. I didn't have any direction, but once I got a little information, I figured out how to go through the process. I got my surgeries for free with Medicaid and insurance. New York has the best care for transgender people in the whole country.

I never had a role model. It was always just me wanting to live my truth and be happy, and I live and look in the mirror and see what I always saw internally.

My advice to anyone transitioning is that it is not easy to prepare for and there is no turning back. Money is not going to make you happy; material things are not going to make you happy. Inner peace will make you happy. And part of transitioning is to become happy with who you are, who you want to be. My biggest breakthrough moment was not the hormones or the surgeries, or even when my father called me his son; it was when I got my name changed. I had this attorney bring me into a nice, savvy office and I had to sign like eight different copies of government-document, name-change papers. That was a big realization of accomplishment and a very happy feeling for me.

—*Seven King*

"We're sisters and we're both trans. Imagine that! We're very proud of it. We inspire each other and we've been great support for each other, which is really important for someone transitioning, especially for one's mental health."

—ANGEL CASTILLO

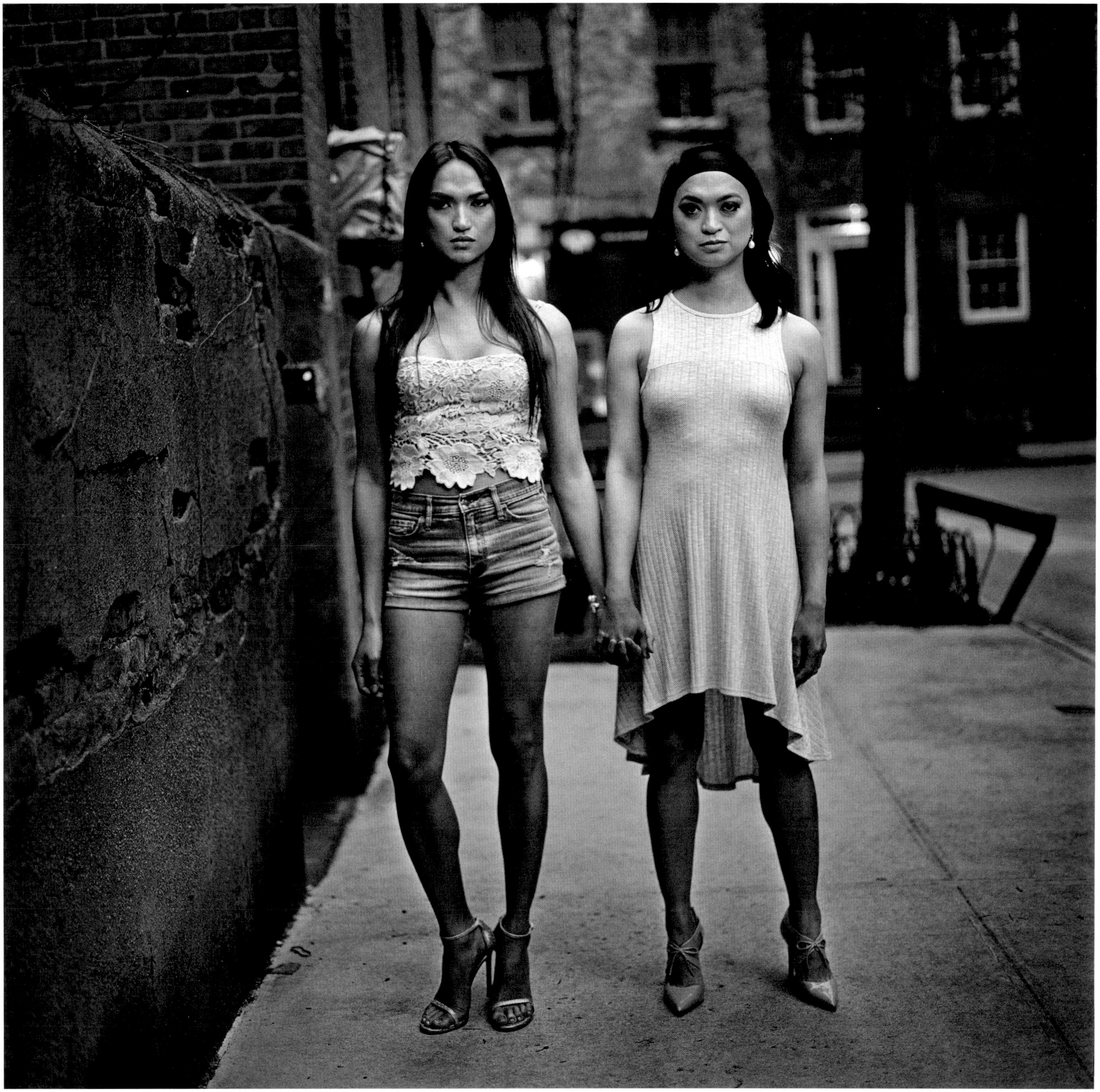

ANGEL CASTILLO AND ALLY CASTILLO

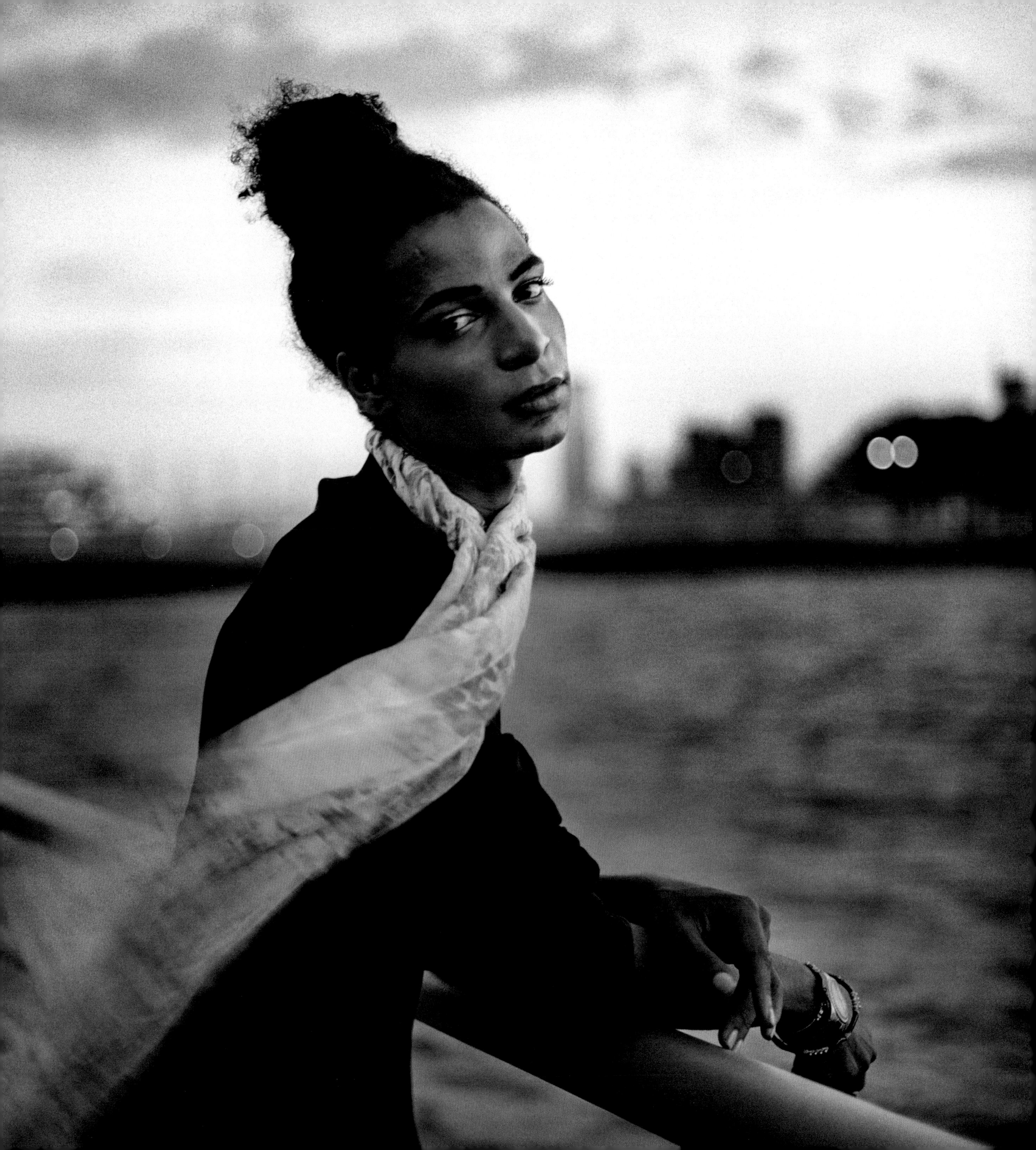

"At the Stonewall last night, a trans woman was sexually assaulted. Even in the most accepting place you can imagine, as a trans person, it's still dangerous. It's important to know that we still have a ways to go."

— GEENA ROCERO

“For close to a decade, I was modeling, and my agent didn’t know I was trans. I was living my dream, but at the same time I was in this constant state of paranoia and fear.”

—GEENA ROCERO

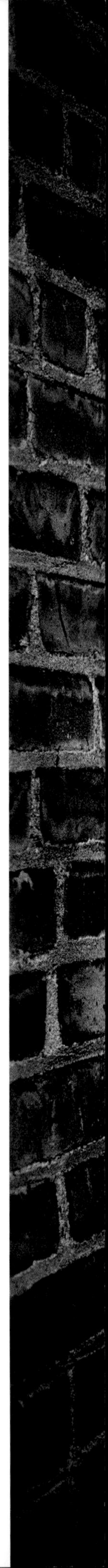

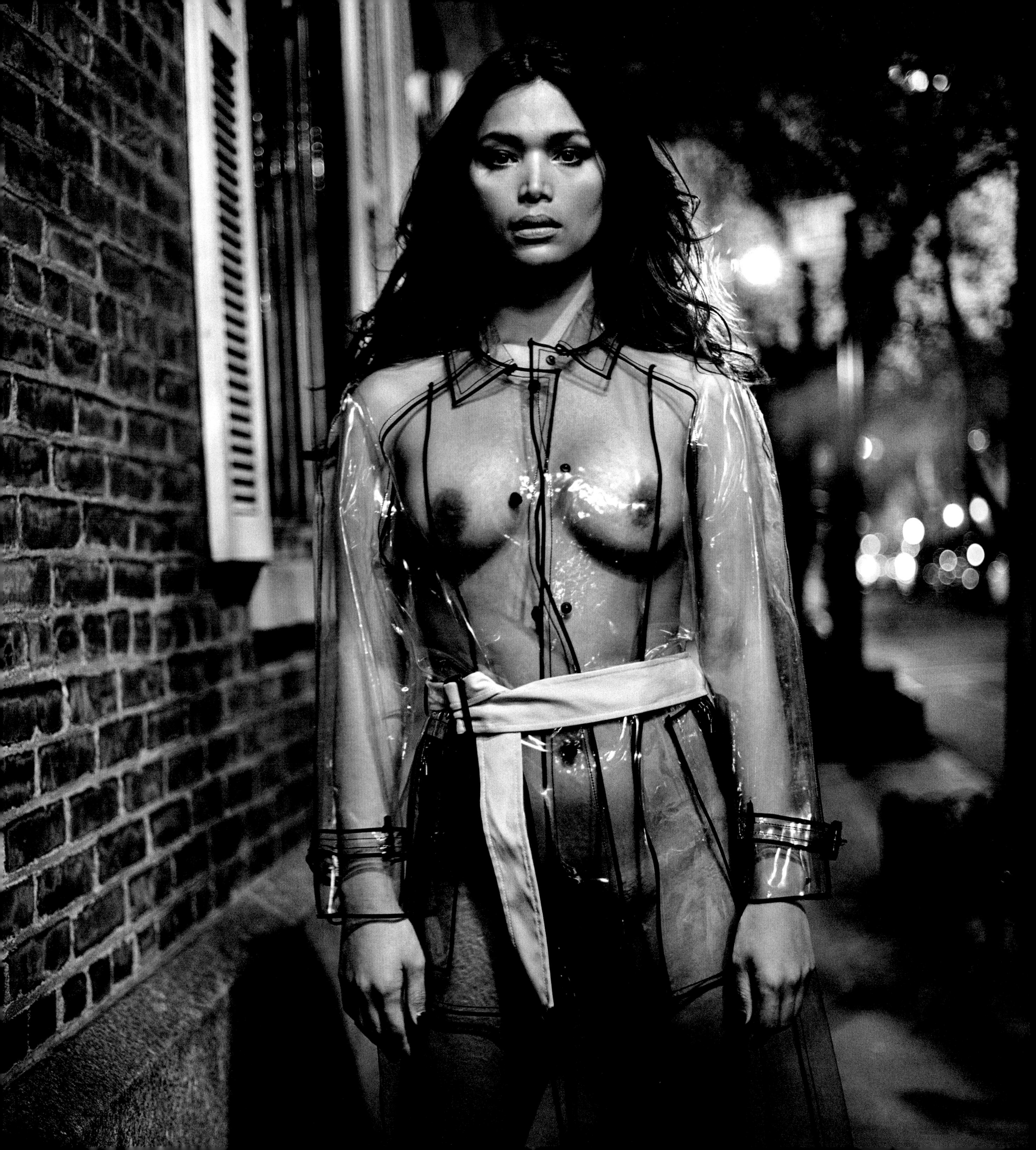

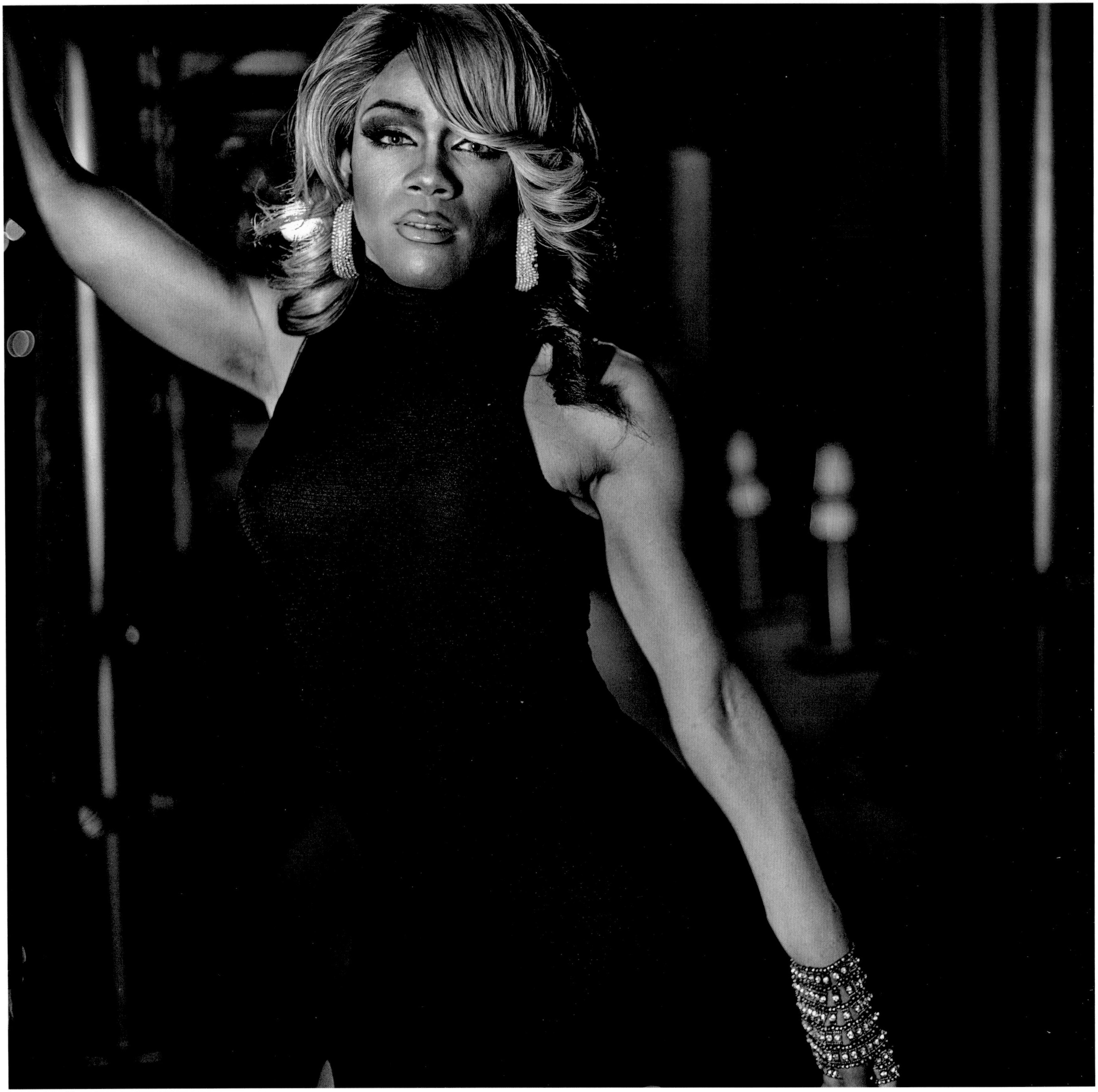

"Dating life as a transgender woman is complicated because one minute a man can be in love with you and the next minute he's in denial."

—EVE BLACK

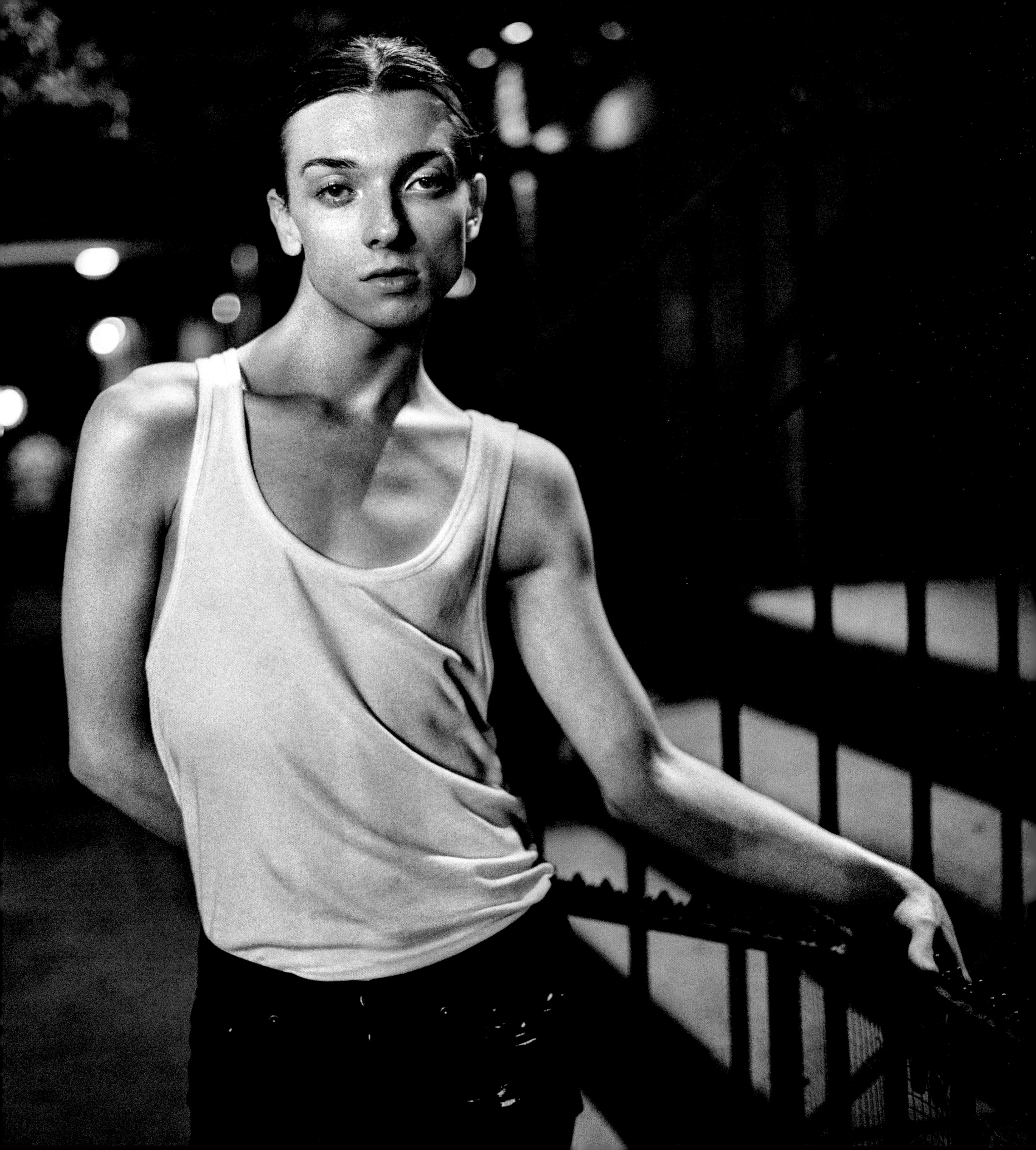

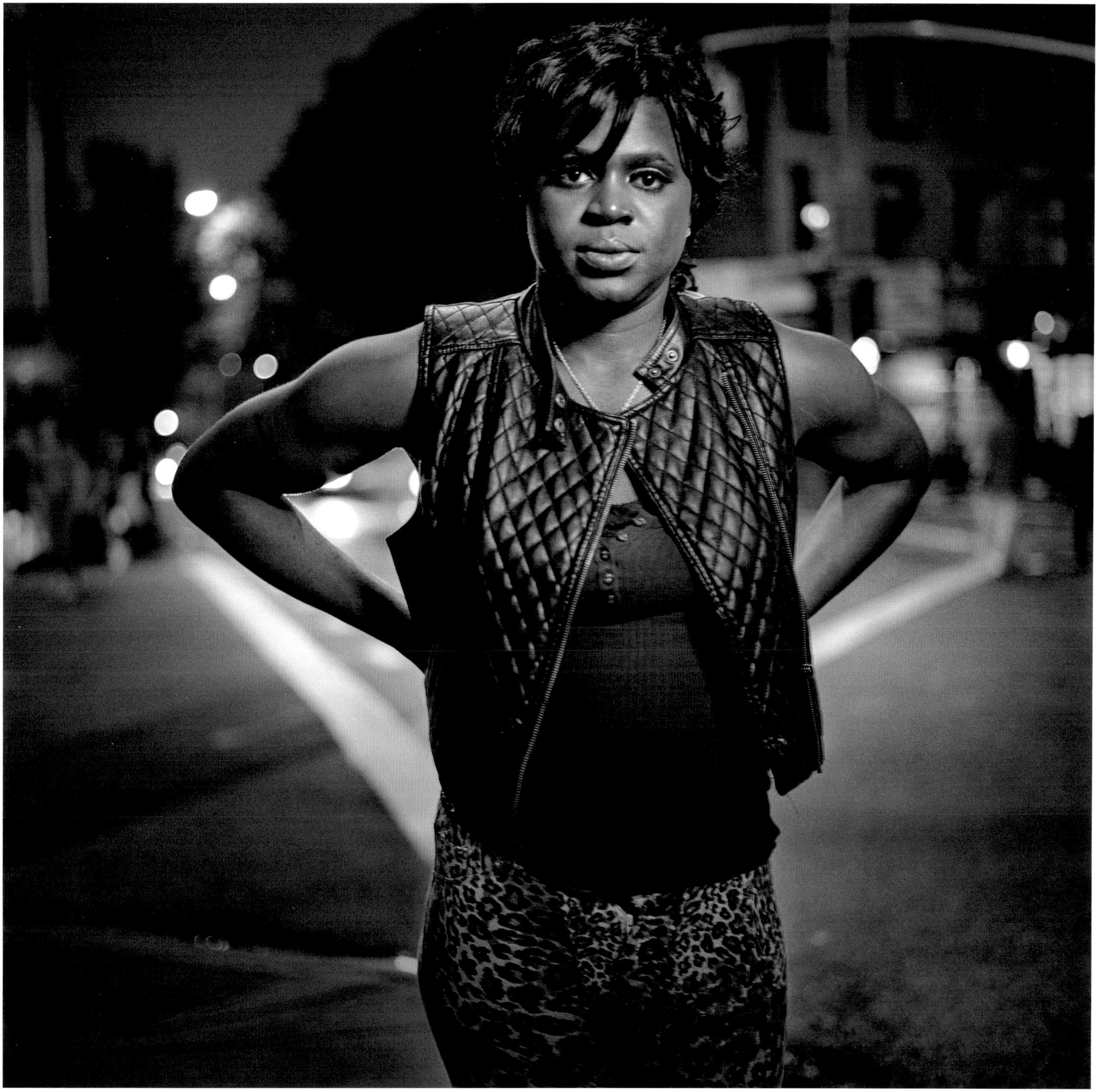

AMBER

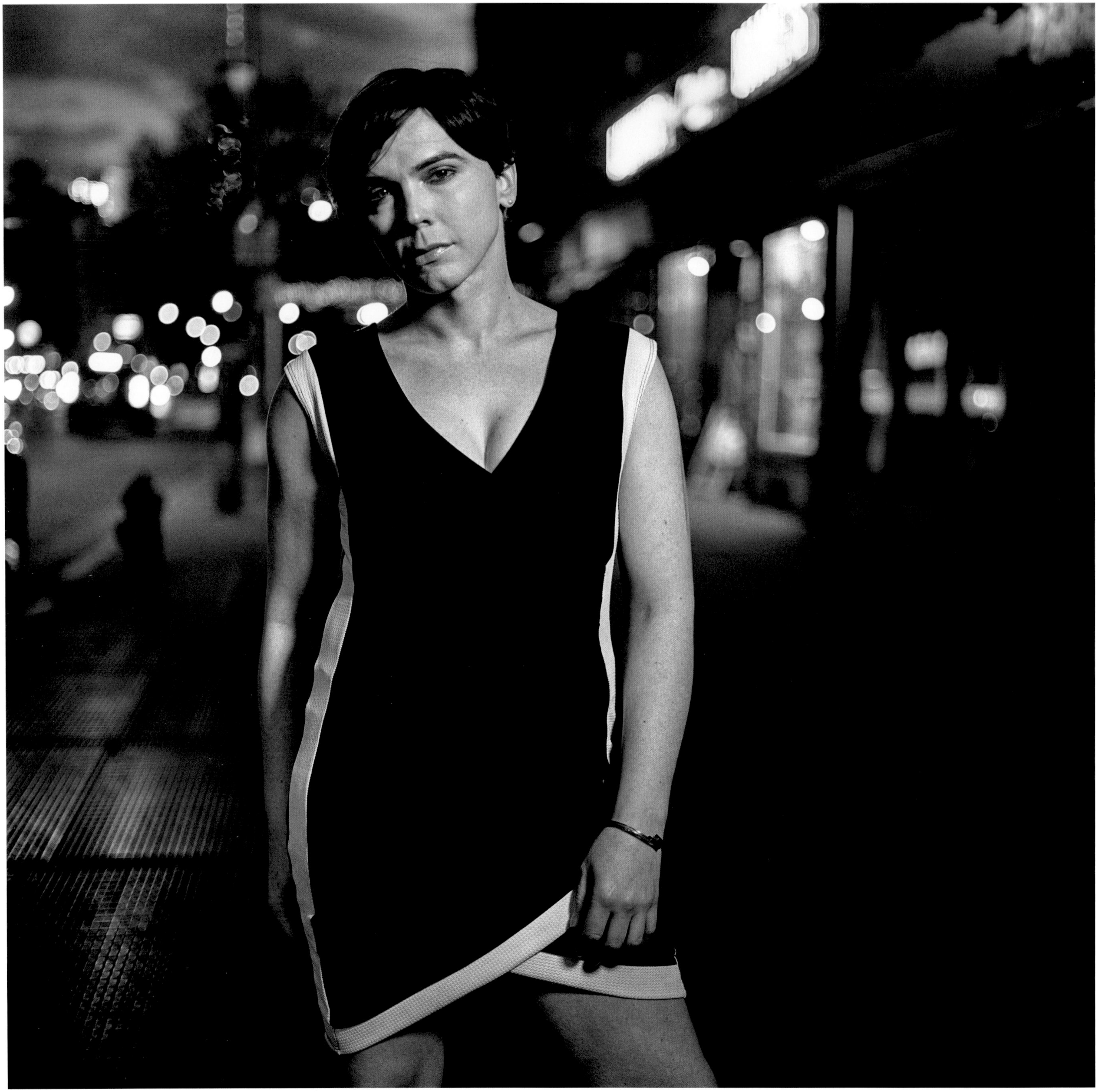

"In a world that is very much heterosexist, patriarchal, and misogynistic, I firmly believe that being trans is resistance."

—LUCKY S. MICHAELS

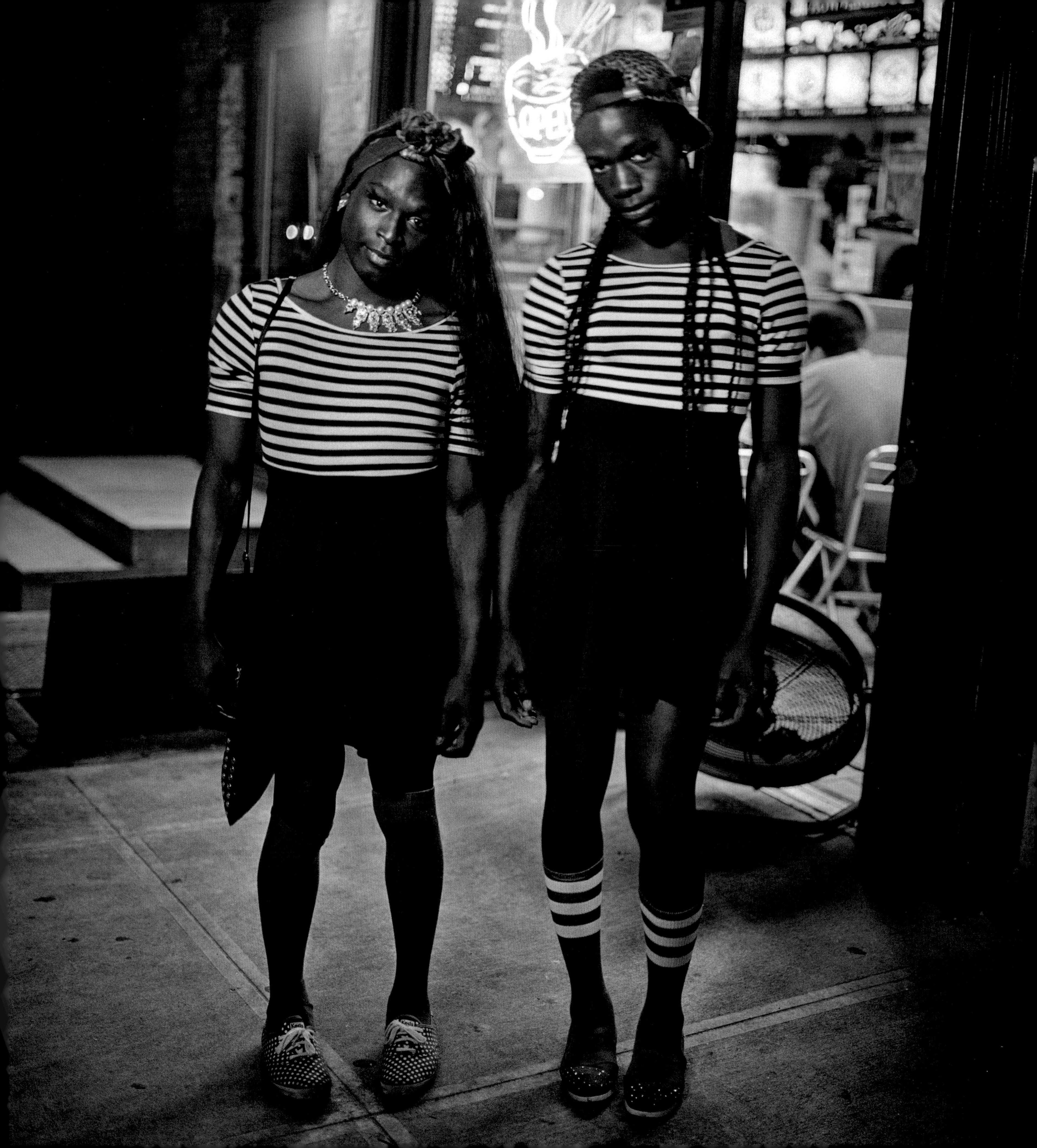

"I am in a relationship. I have a boyfriend. His name is Sam. We've been together for almost three years. We live together in Brooklyn. We just adopted a dog."

—AMOS MAC

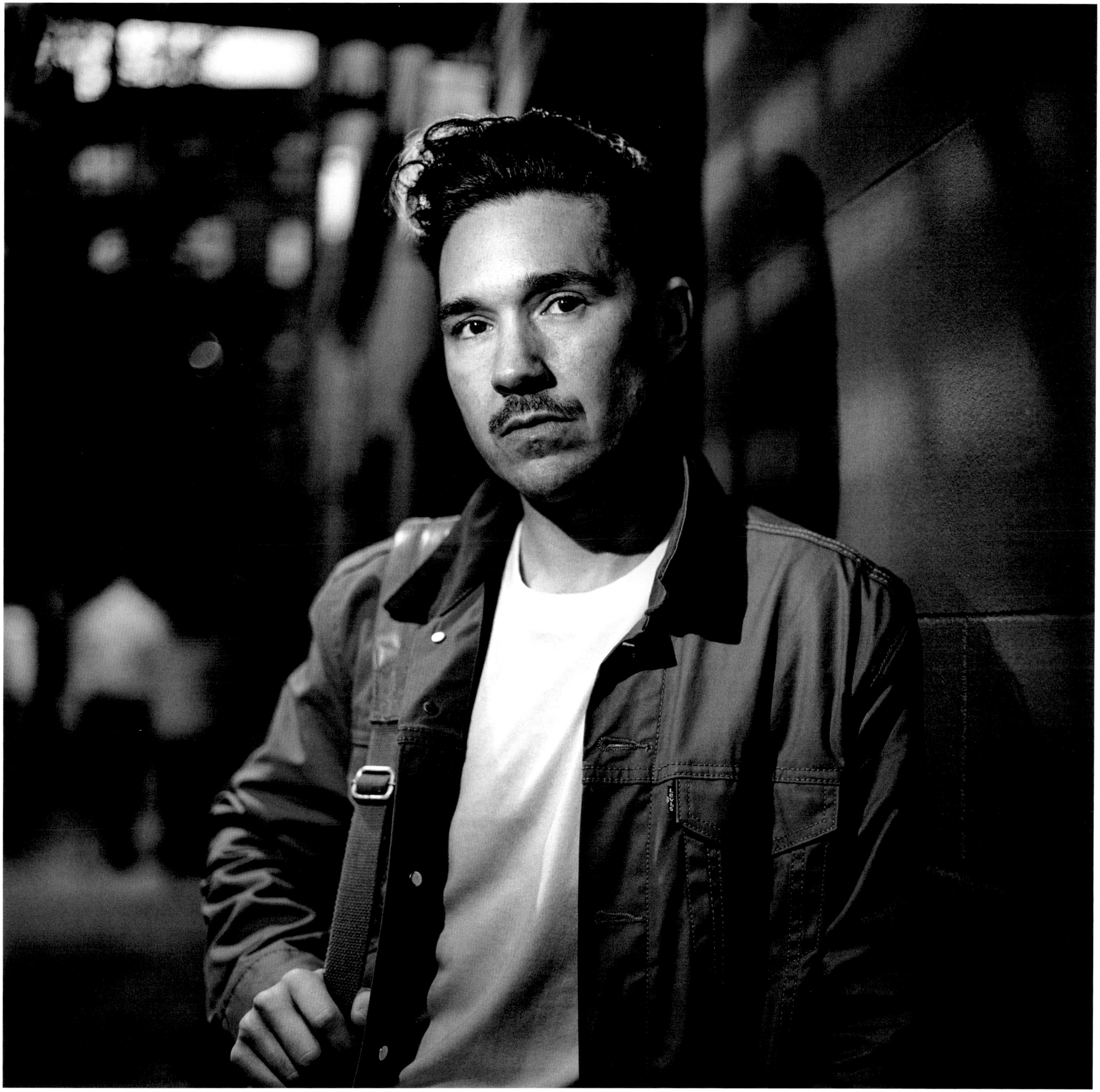

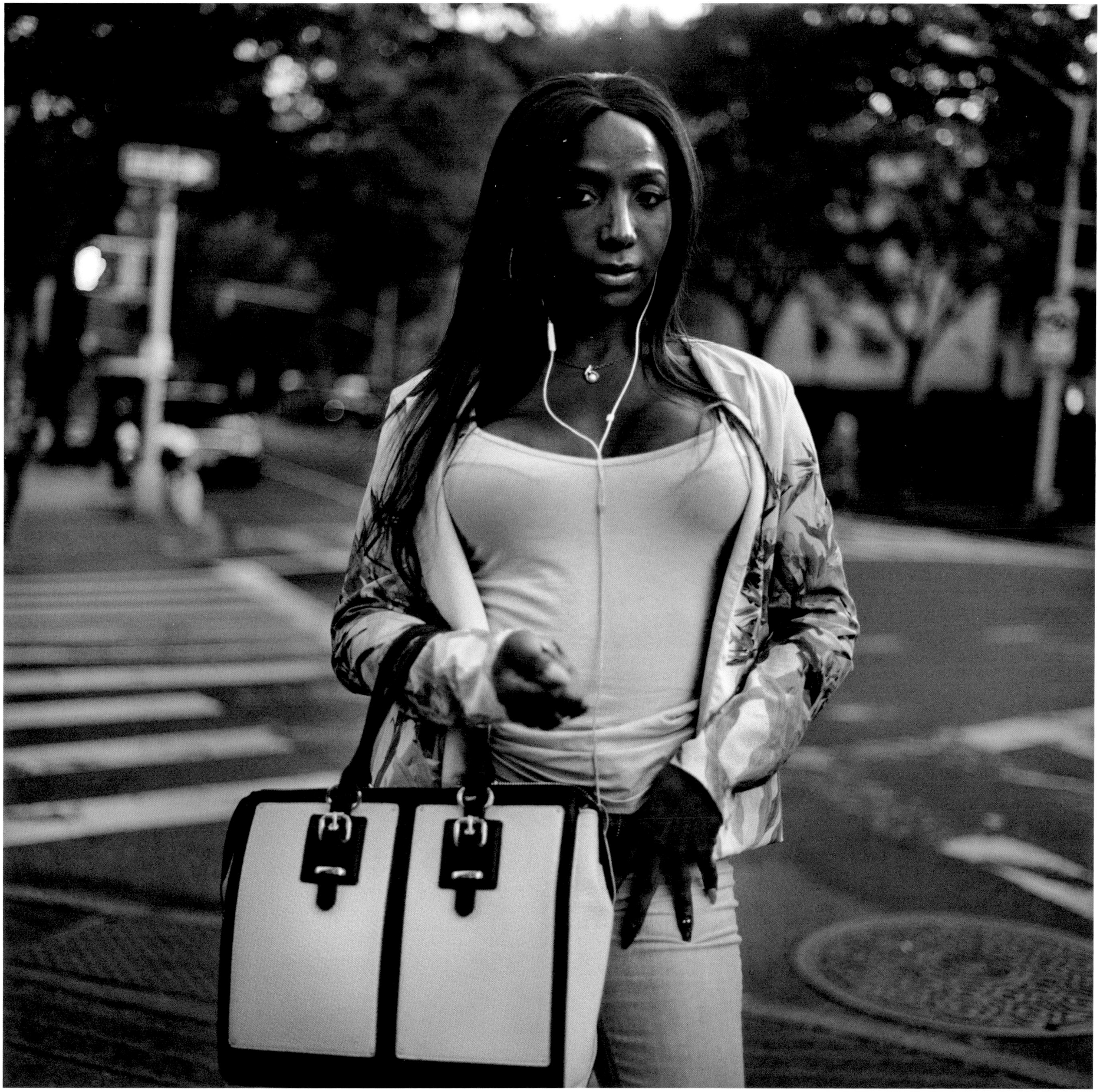

CHANTEL ARMANI SHAVERS

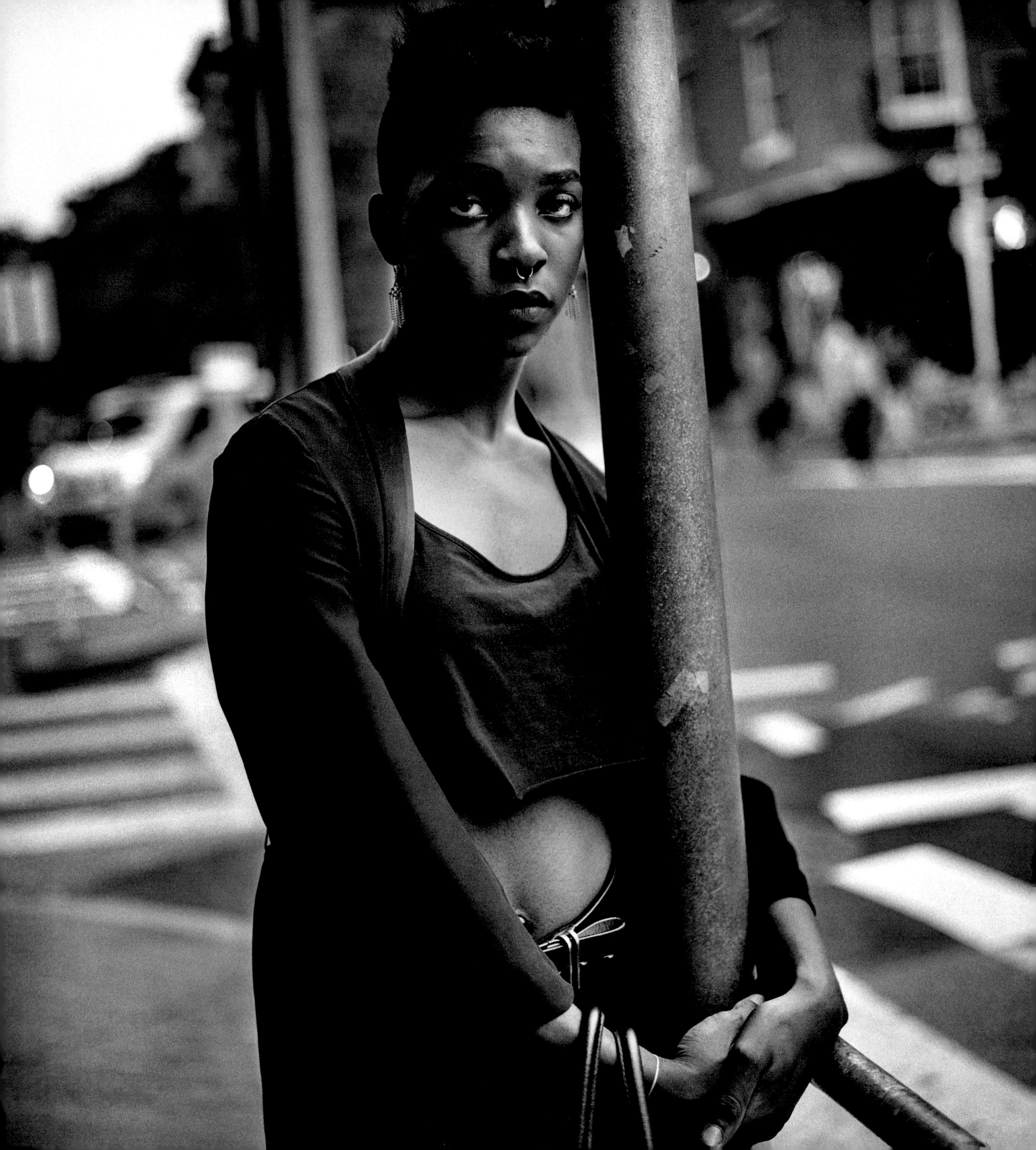

"Some people are gender nonconforming, or choose no gender at all, because that is how they are comfortable. If you want to present as male one day and female another, that should be your prerogative. Society puts people in boxes. You have to be male or female. And you shouldn't. You should just have to be human."

— JEVON MARTIN

"The only relationship my transition really affected was my relationship with my daughter. She always wanted a girly mother, and that wasn't me. And she wanted me to dress more feminine. That wasn't me, either. To this day, she still has several little qualms with the way I am. But she has finally come to terms with the fact that I am male. And she calls me Pop. She calls me Jevon. She calls me J. But she won't call me Dad because I'm not her father. She has a father, and I'm good with that."

—JEVON MARTIN

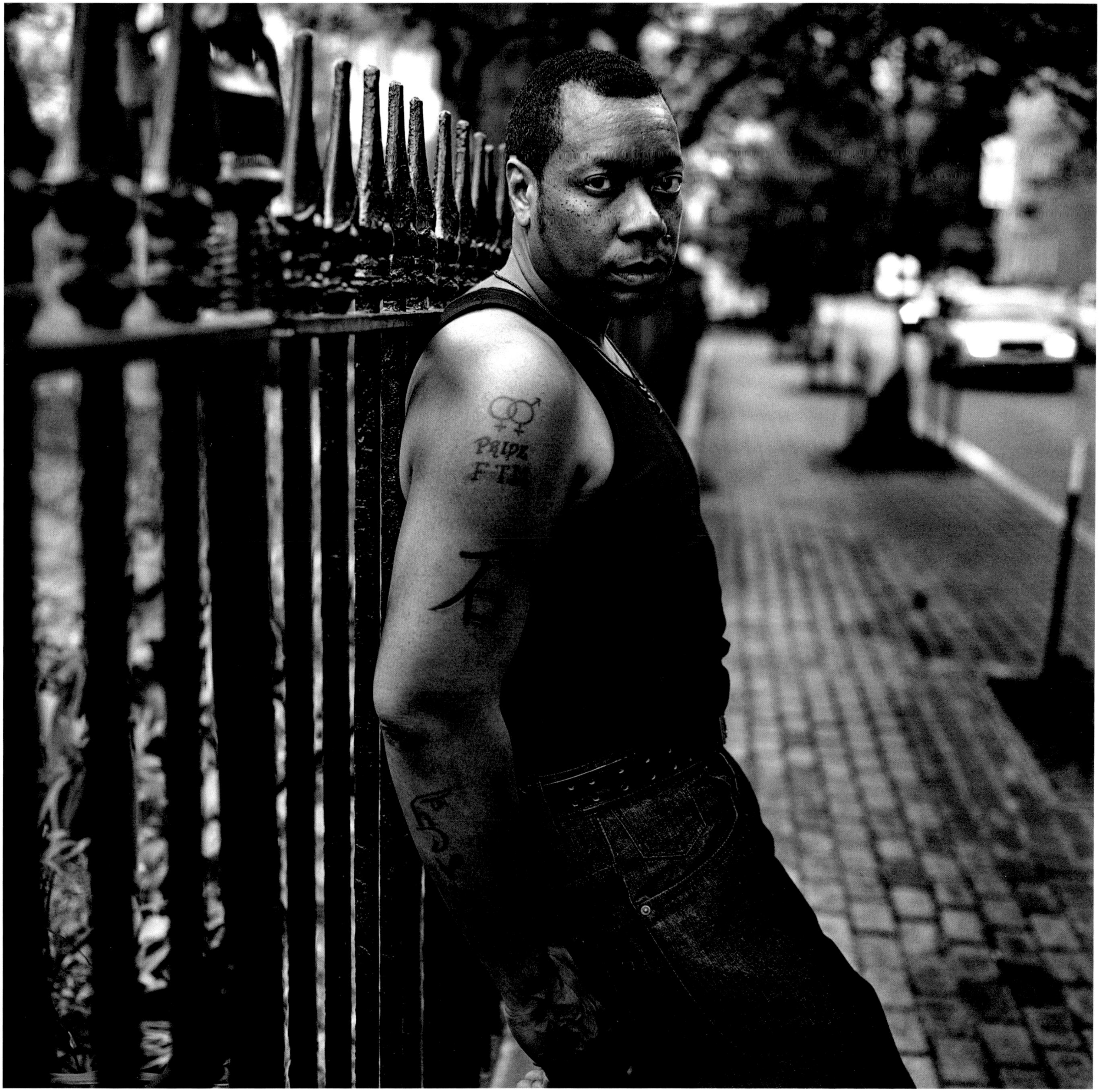

JEVON MARTIN

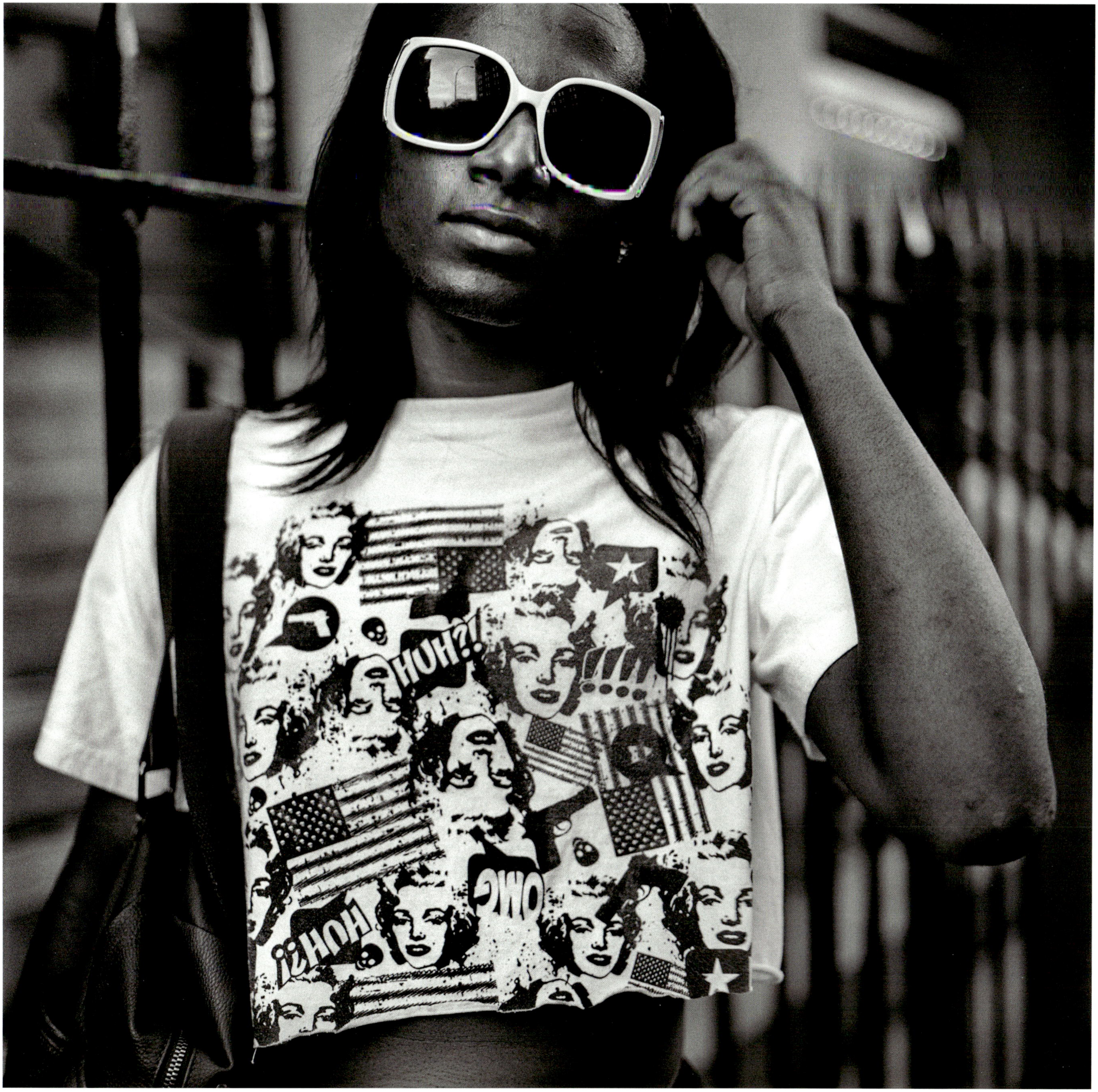

ISIAH

"I realized that I was in the wrong body when I was about four. I used to say a prayer every night before going to bed, asking that when I wake up and look in the mirror, I would see a girl staring back at me. I would say that prayer over and over. I always remember that."

—STEFANIE RIVERA

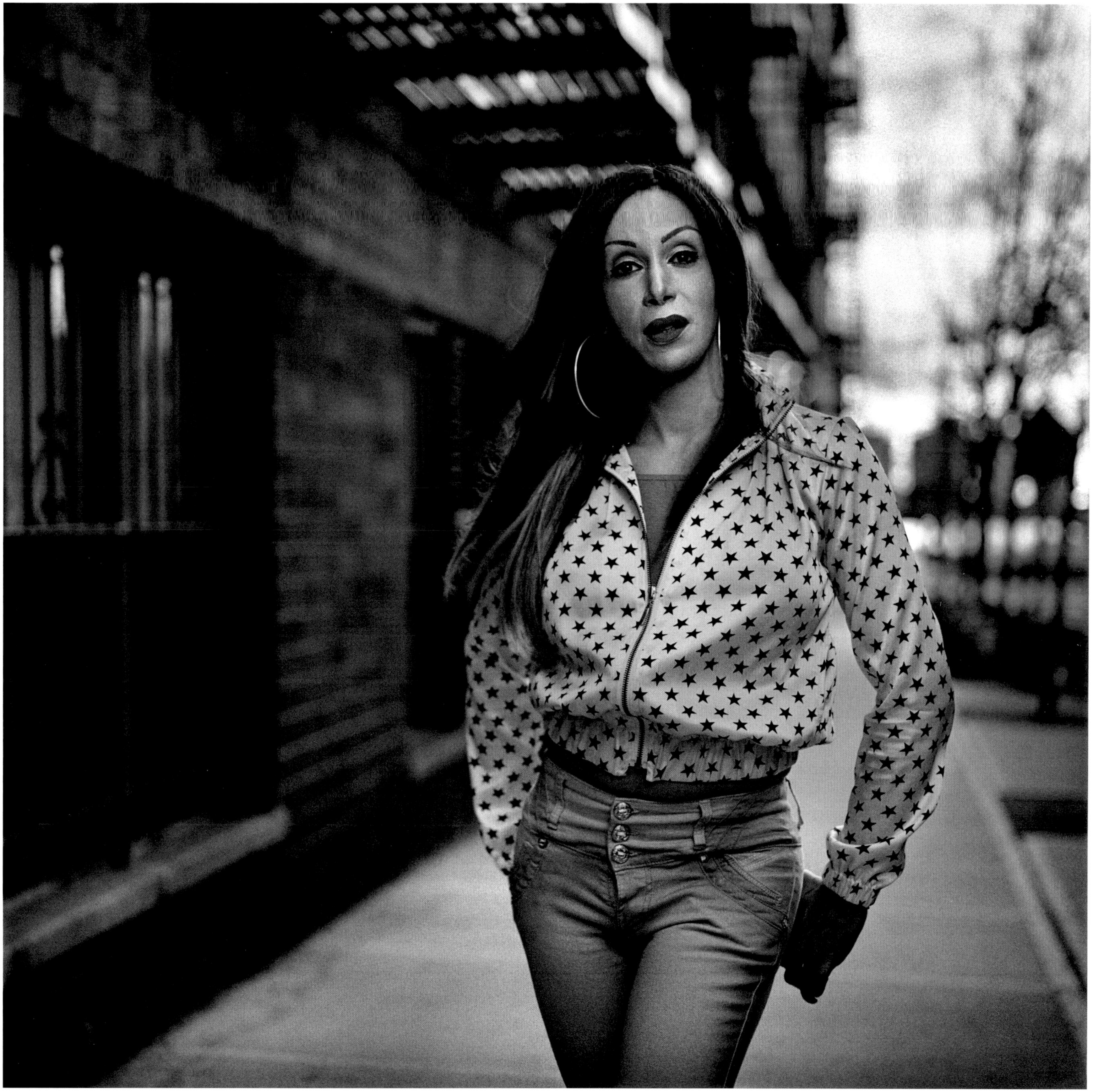

I'M ORIGINALLY FROM BOSTON, MASSACHUSETTS, and now I live in New York City. I was raised Greek Orthodox and I remember the first time I felt different in my body—I was around ten, and my family and I were getting ready to go to church and I really did not want to wear a dress. I wanted to wear a suit. I really wanted to look like the Greek composer Yanni. I wanted his suit and his hair. But I knew, because I was assigned female gender at birth and people saw me as female, that I couldn't achieve that. I was so young. I didn't know the name for what I was.

When I was in college, before I physically transitioned, as I was figuring stuff out, I really looked up to Leslie Feinberg, who wrote *Stone Butch Blues*. She worked a lot for labor rights and economic equality and really paved the way for trans men to investigate their masculinity. When I transitioned, at twenty-three, it was a revelatory moment because it was really like a cloud lifting off me. Leading up to that moment was a lot of darkness and even attempted suicide. I finally realized that I had to physically transition in order to survive and be myself. So after months and years of depression, it was amazing to transition. But it was also nerve-wracking because I didn't know what to expect: from taking injections of hormones to how I'd actually look and what to tell my family. I knew my life would never be the same.

I remember when I told my parents, over the phone, my heart wouldn't stop beating. I explained, the best I could, that the reason I had been struggling for so many years wasn't because I was confused about my sexuality; it was because I wasn't in the right body. As I was explaining this, my mom just hung up the phone. My parents kind of disowned me for two years. I went to a trans masculine support group near Christopher Street, and that's where all my trans male friends come from. So I can't separate Christopher Street from my transition—they go hand in hand. When I didn't have family for two years, my friends from the support group became my family.

The tension with my parents resolved itself in 2013, when I had been on T for two years. My mom came to New York, and we spent Christmas together and she bought me some shaving products. It was a radical shift. Shortly thereafter, my dad came around as well, and we're actually closer now. You wouldn't think this guy from Iran, originally, would be that way, but he's done his research and he's come a long way, even supporting me through my surgery goals.

I think there is a misconception. People see Caitlyn Jenner and they think it was an overnight transition, but in reality, it had taken her a while to get to where she is now. There are many steps. Trans men usually start with testosterone. You get your first shot of T and you see how you like it. I got facial hair almost right away, and I loved the changes. After about a year, I got top surgery. Usually, people will start out getting hormones first and then get surgeries as well, if they want to do that—hormones, top surgery, hysterectomy. And then, for me, I'll have the full phalloplasty. My approach was to take it slow and let my body recover and not jump into things. It's a social, as well as an emotional, transition.

When people see trans people or hear trans stories, there is often confusion. The way I describe it is that being trans is about your body, and your sexuality is about who you are attracted to. That's the best way I can explain gender versus sexuality. I am and always have been attracted to women—that never changed for me. But for some other trans people, they might explore different sexualities. I would say there's a lot of fluidity inside the trans community, just like there is outside the trans community.

—Tony Zosherafatain

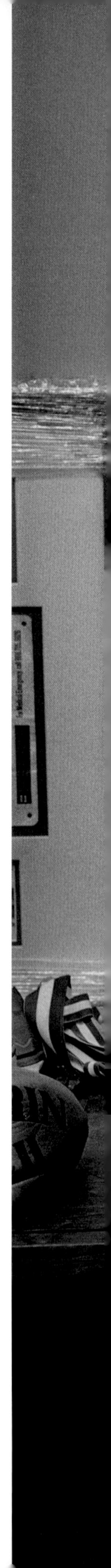

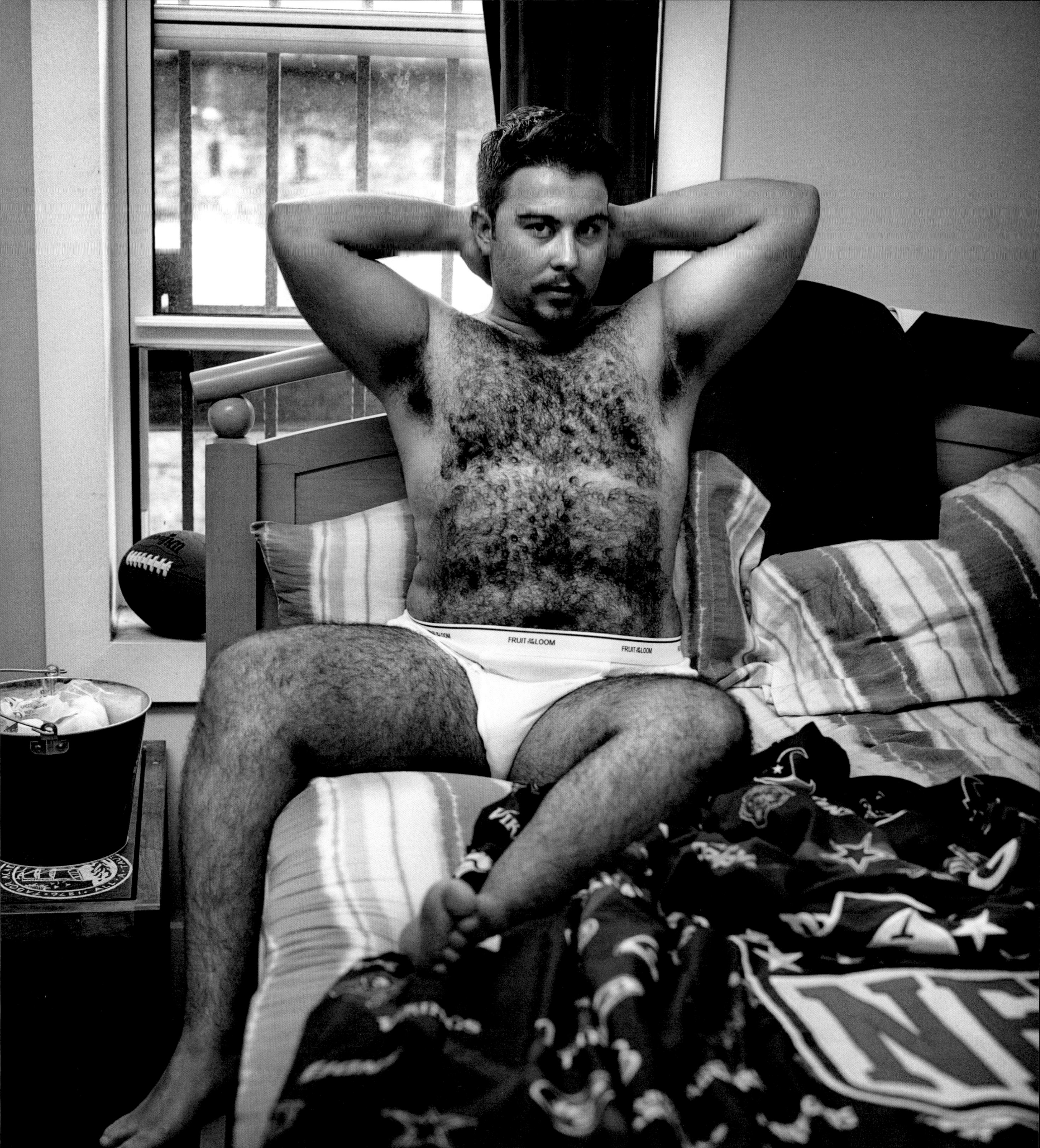

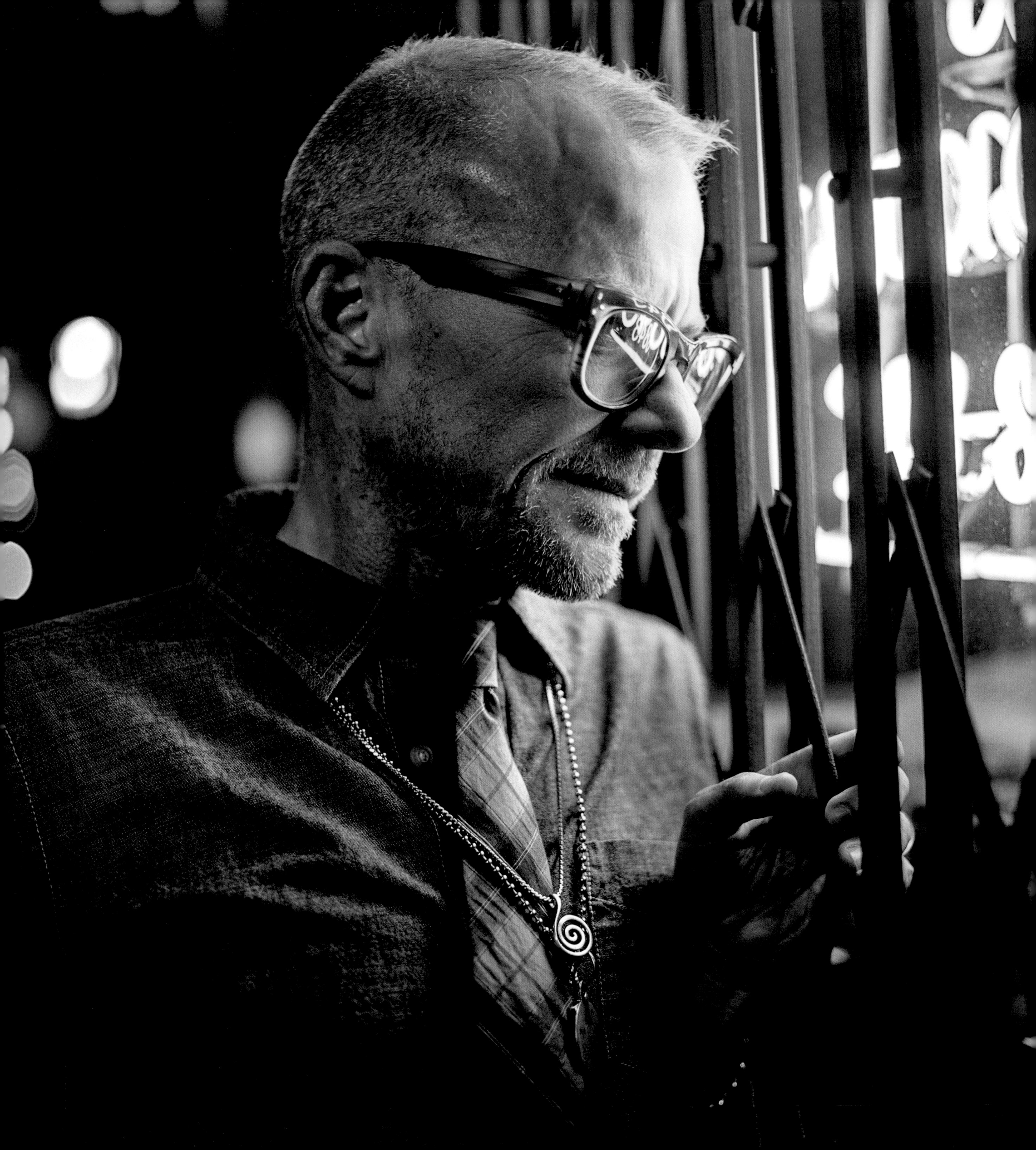

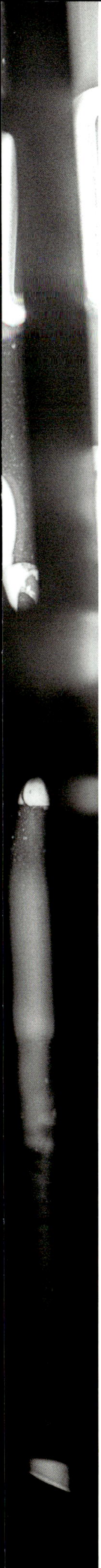

"I always wanted to be a boy—always. I don't remember ever not wanting that."

—LES LARUE

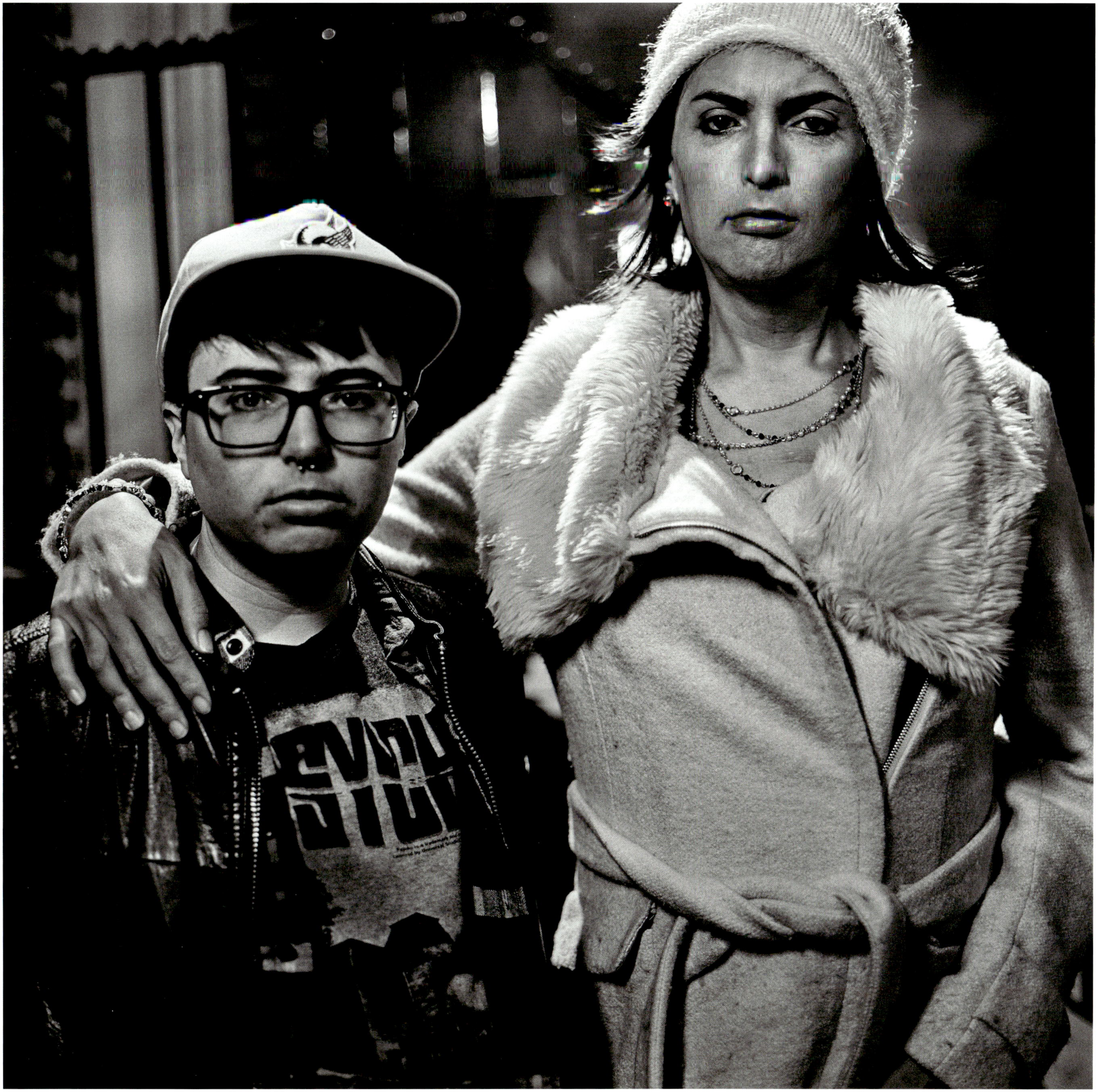

FELIX HYDE AND JEENA HYDE [SIBLINGS]

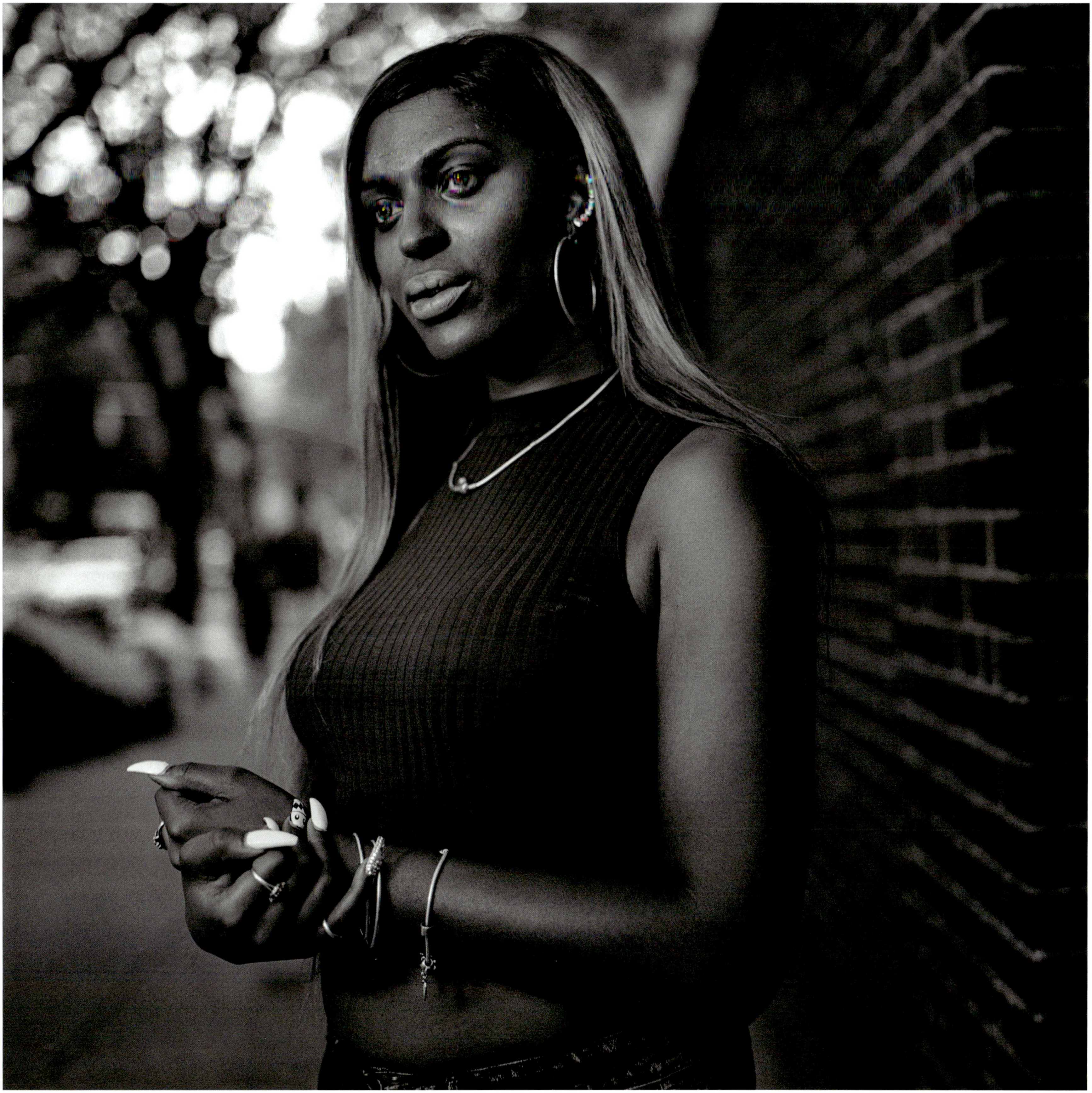

"I knew I was different, probably at four or five years old, but I didn't do anything about it until last year. My wife and I decided to divorce, and we have two sons—one is nineteen and one is seventeen—and obviously it has been difficult. But it was as if, once I became Bree, all my fears went away. It's been just beautiful."

—BREE BENZ

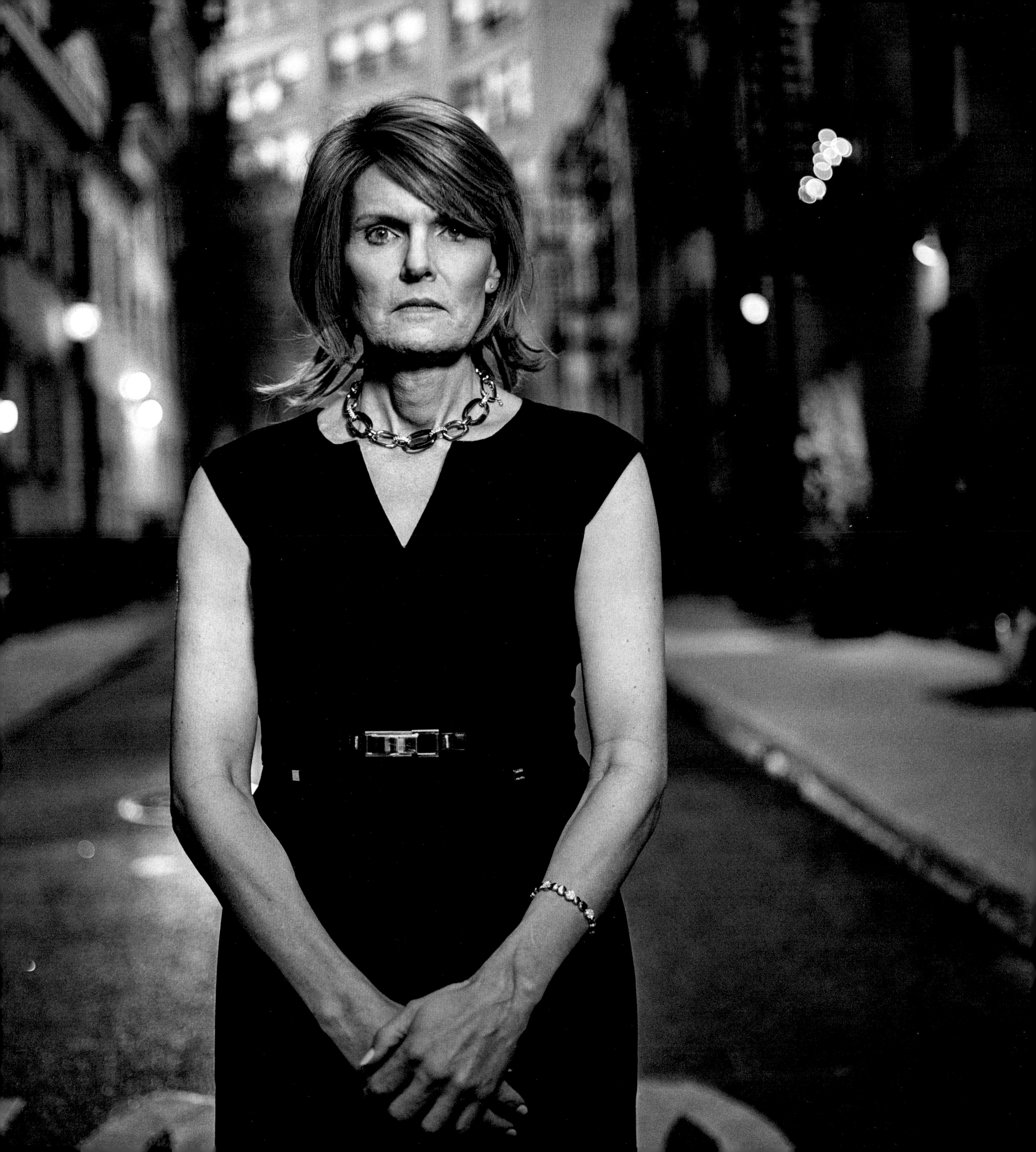

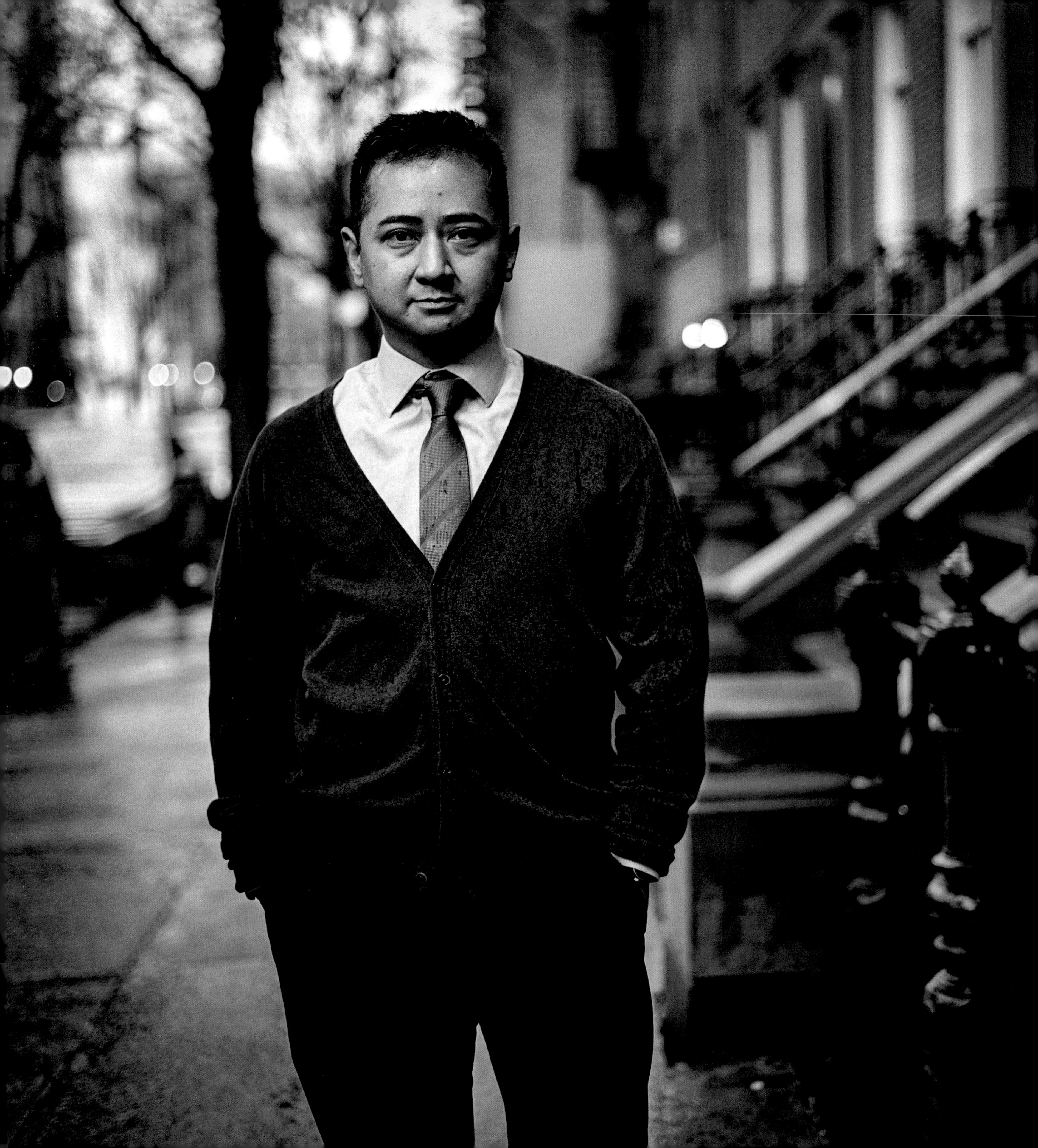

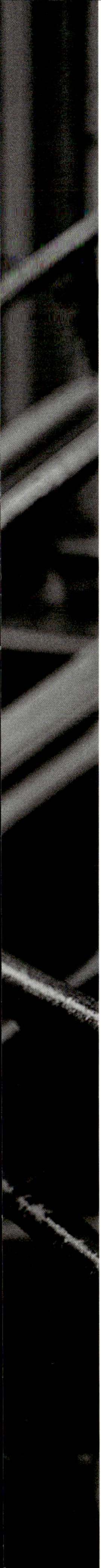

"I've always been a big fan of the Christopher Reeve Superman sweet, approachable, caring, but at the same time strong and respected."

—M. DAVID SOLIVEN

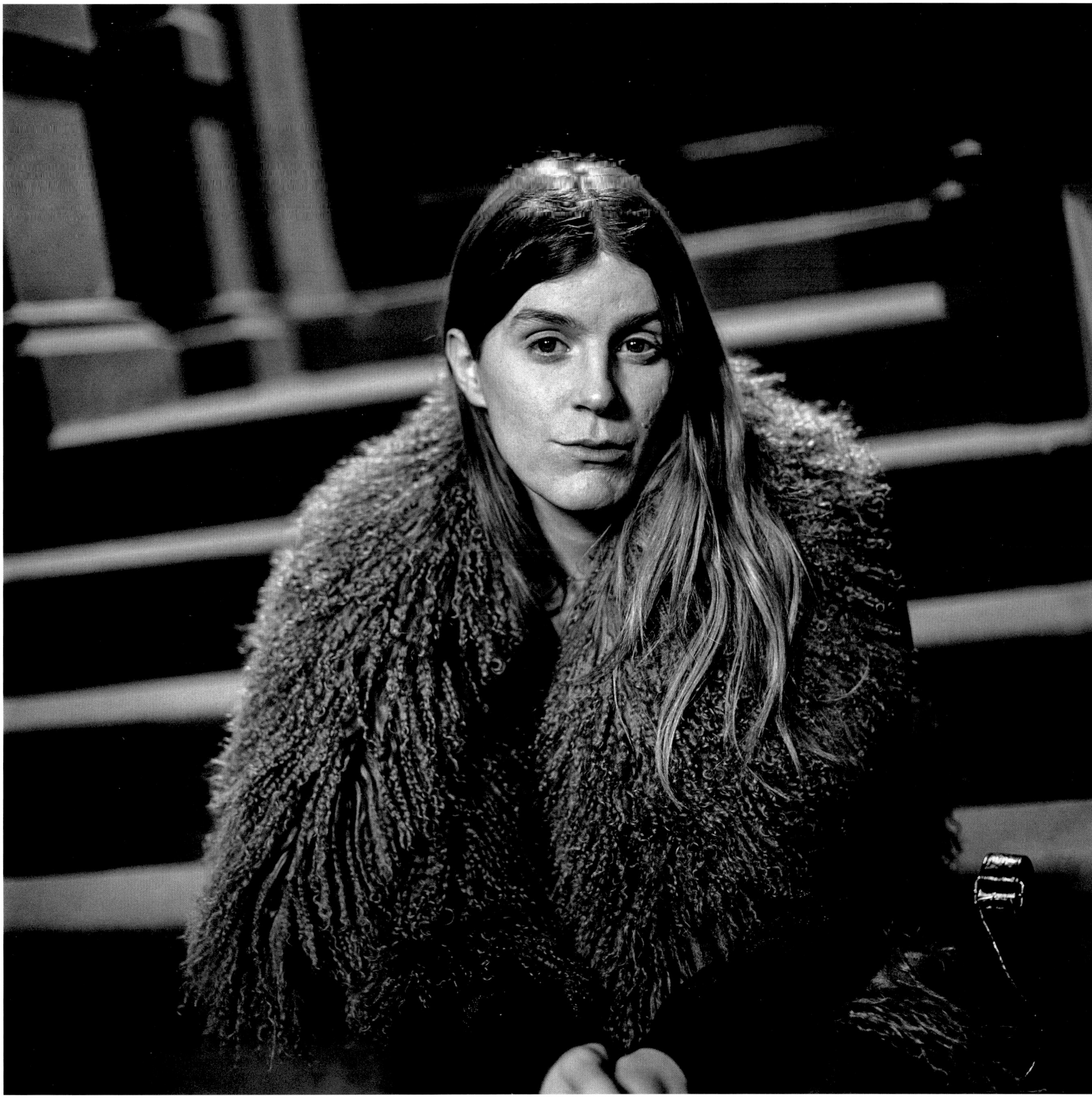

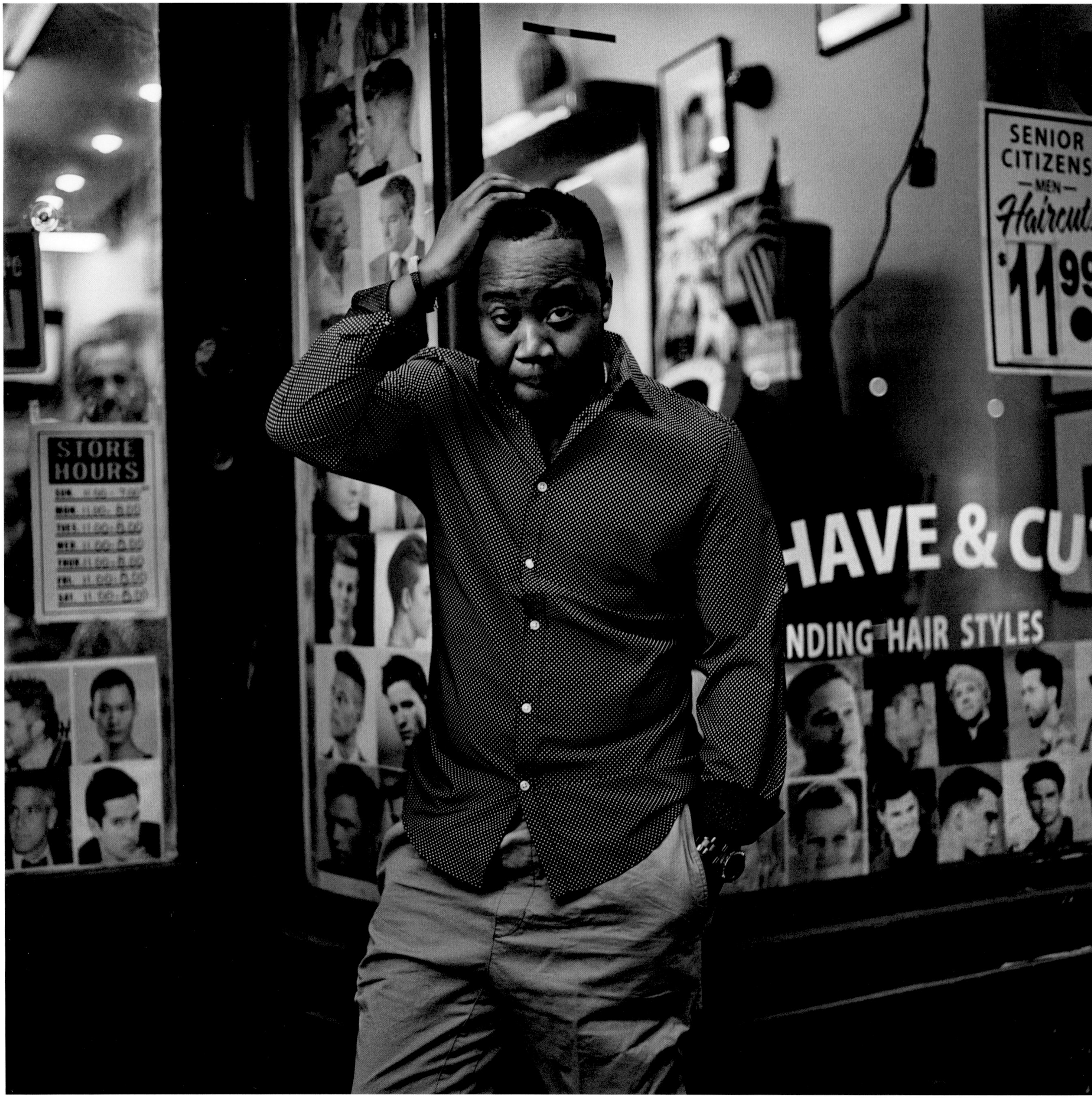
SENIOR
CITIZENS
— MEN —
Haircuts
$11 99
STORE
HOURS
HAVE & CU
NDING HAIR STYLES

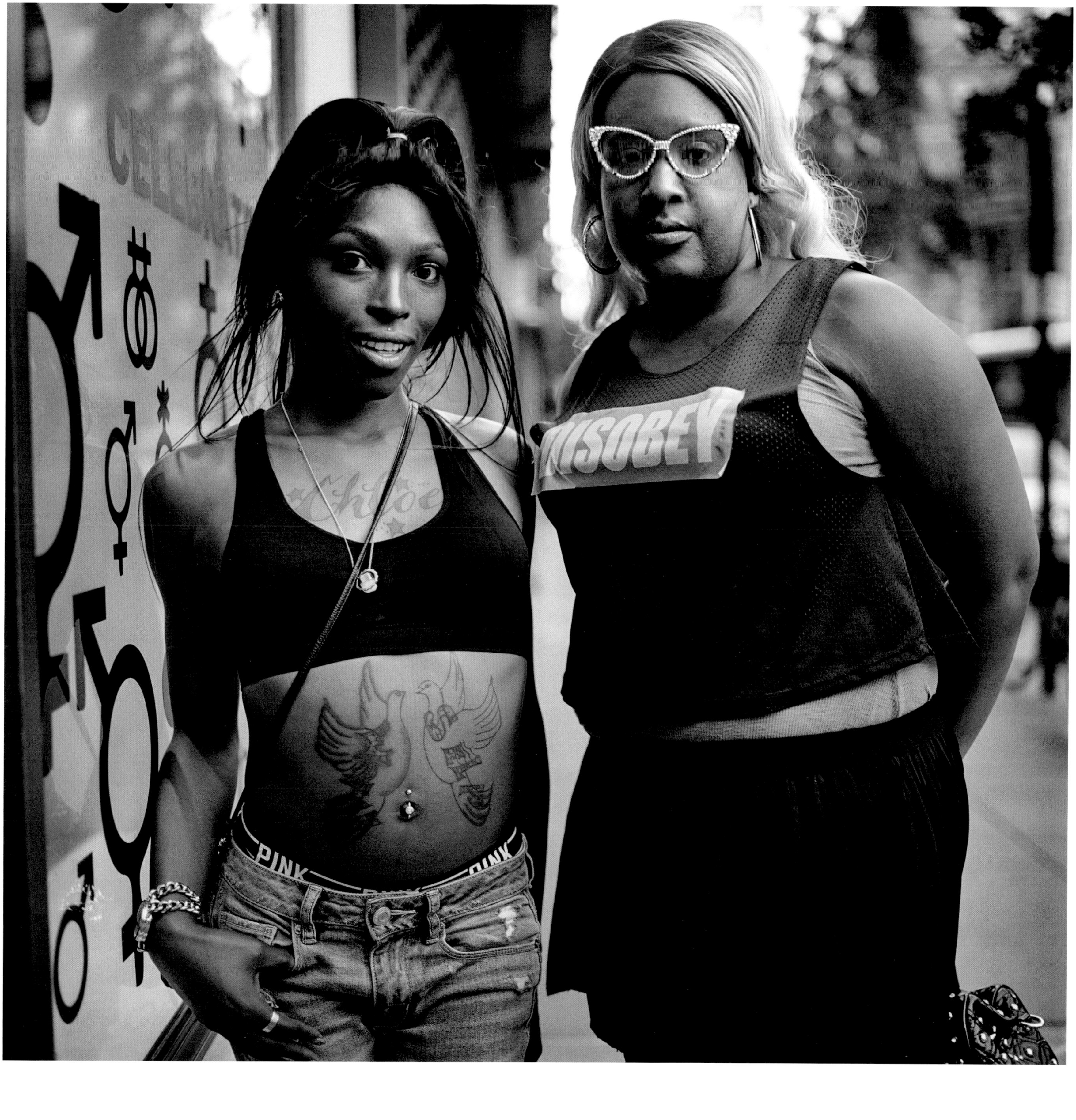

CHLOE MITCHELL AND LALA ZANNELL

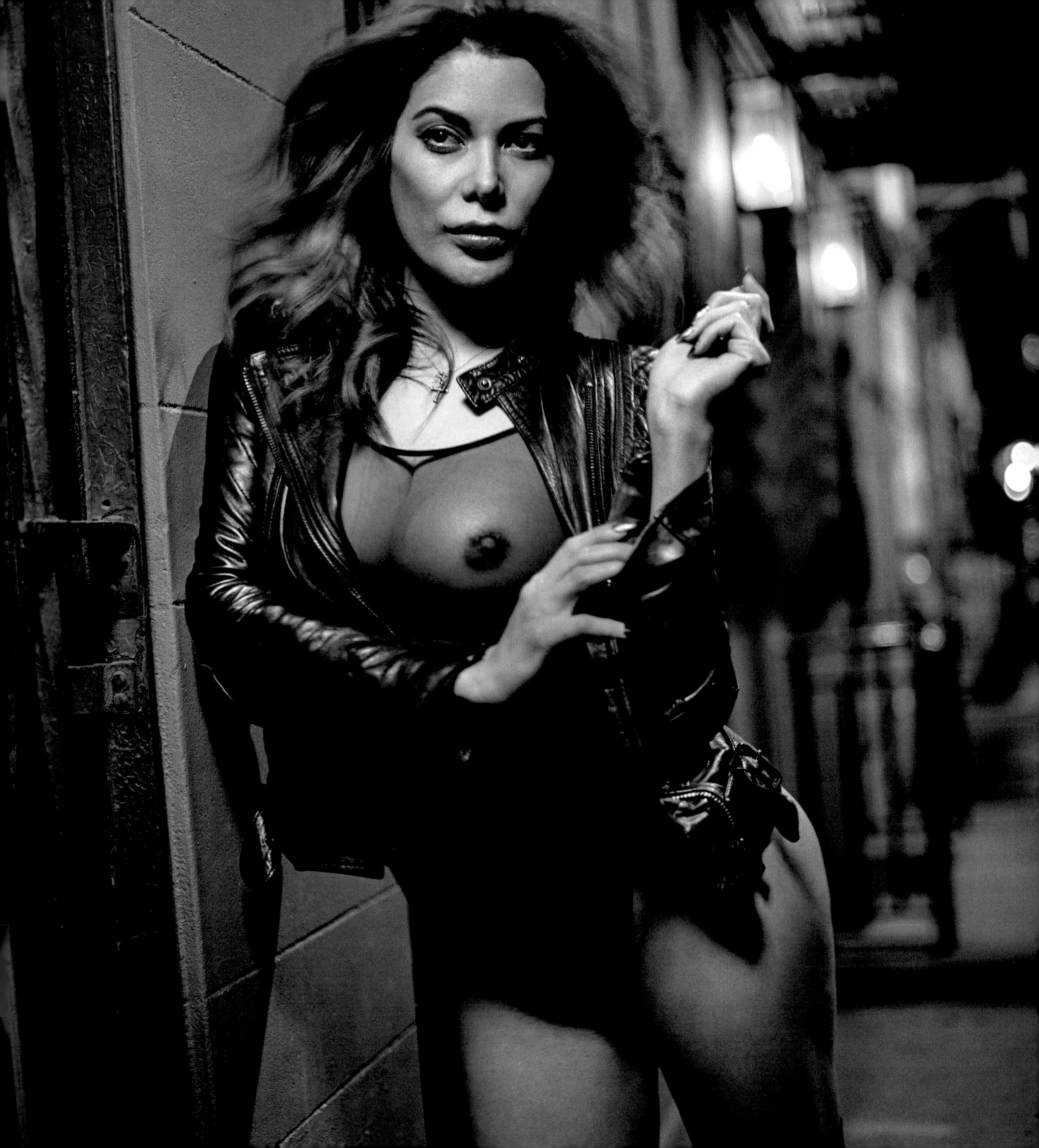

"I did a movie called *The Dictator*, with Sacha Baron Cohen and Ben Kingsley and Megan Fox, and I wasn't out. And the *New York Post* outed me as a transsexual actress, which devastated me. I felt very discriminated against."

— VICTORIA BELTRAN

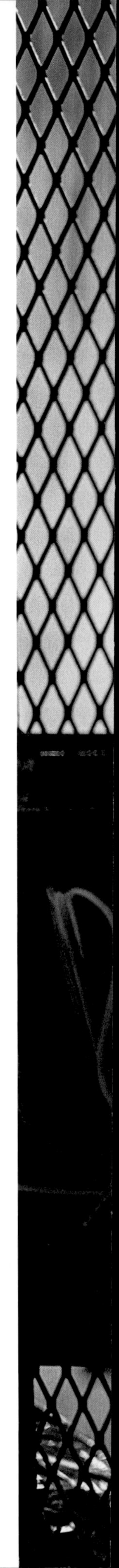

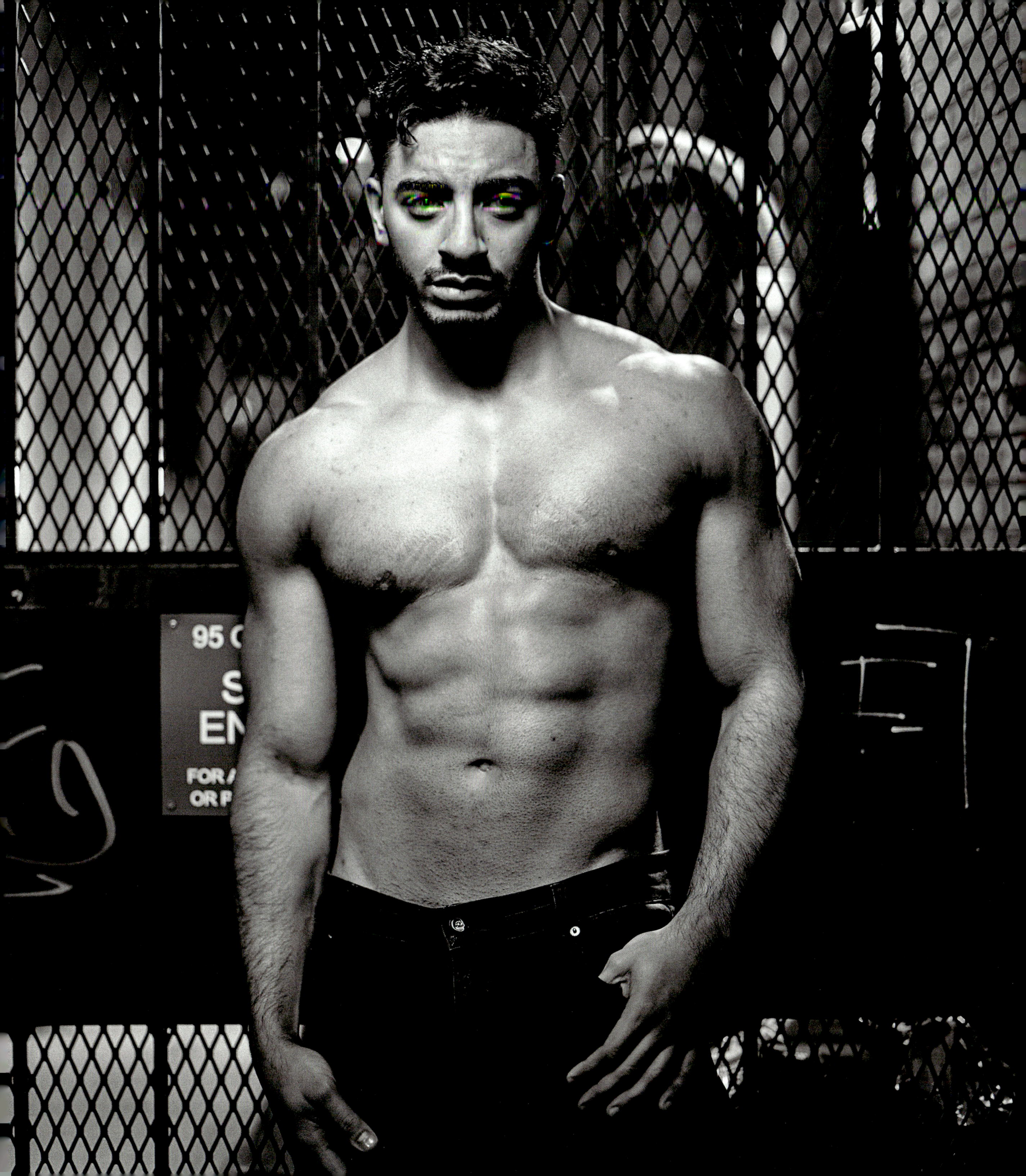

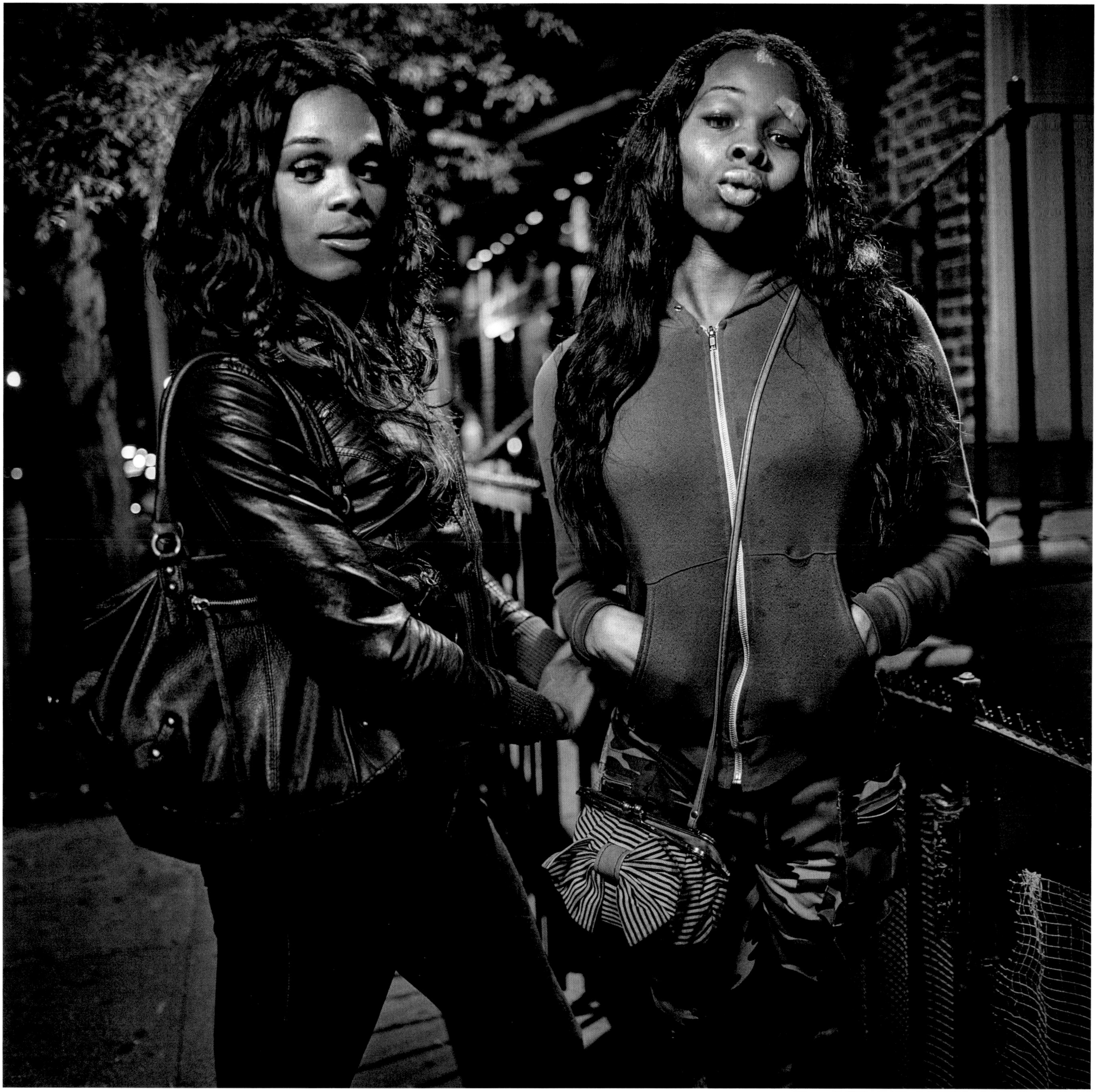

BARBIE KARDASHIAN AND FRIEND

"When I arrived at Christopher Street, it was very scary. There was a train track in the middle of the highway. That pier didn't look like it does now. It was just cars and people doing all kinds of ungodly things. It was scary, but it was also exciting, because it was something new and I saw another part of life. And it made me aware of who I was—a trans woman."

—EGYPTT LABIEJA

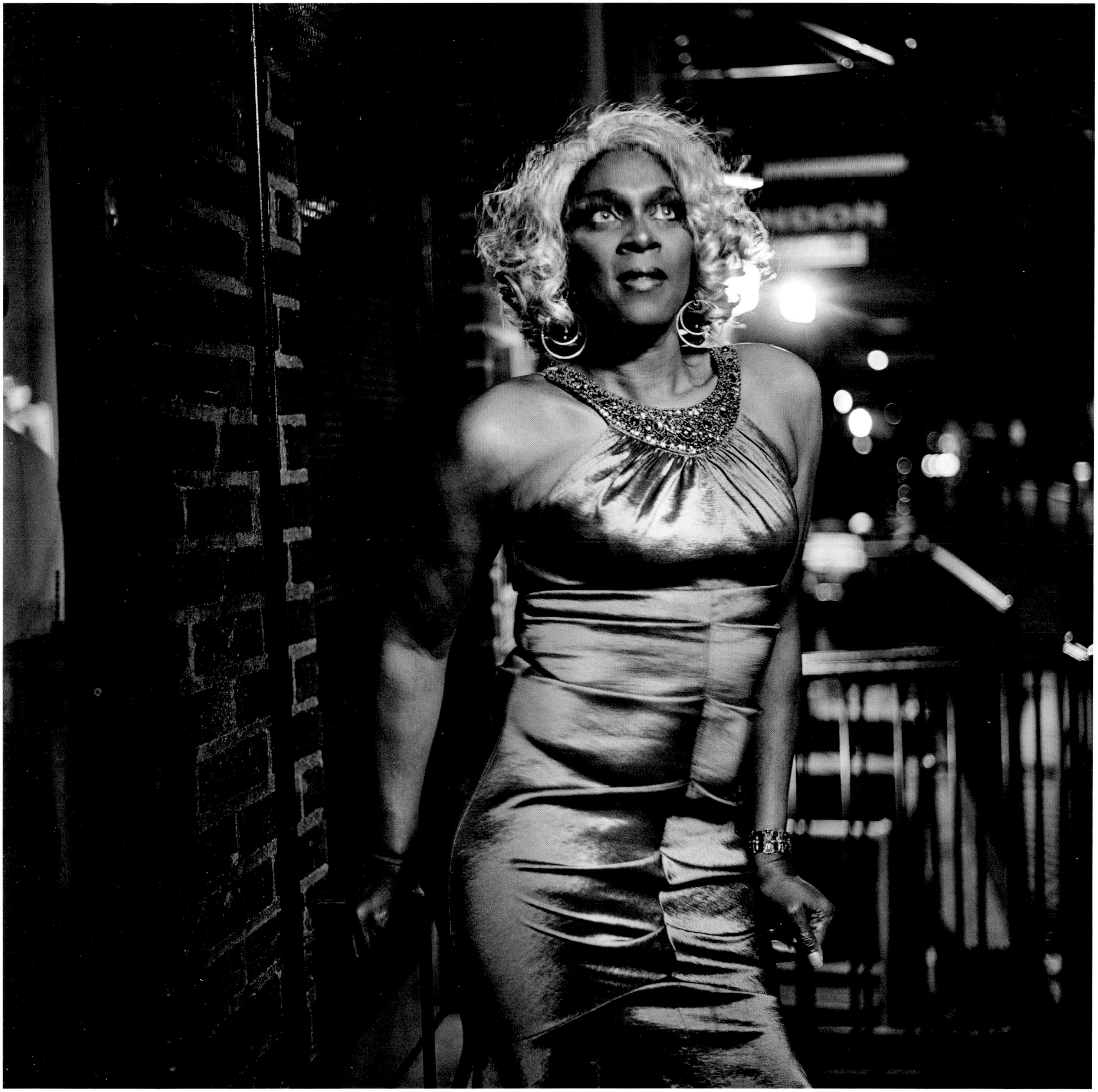

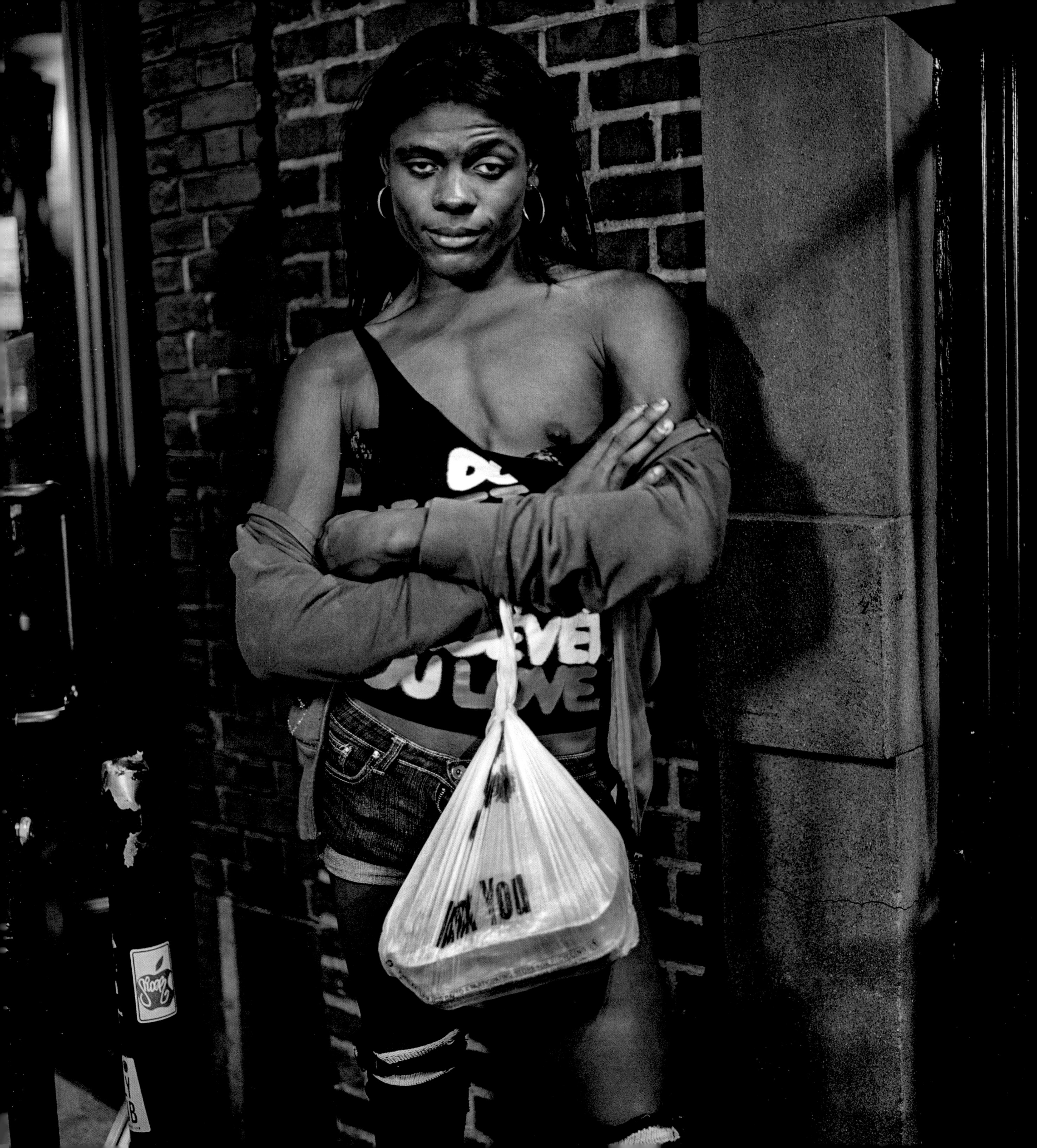
YOU

One wild weekend, I got this tattoo. That was how I felt at the time—invaluable, like, "Fuck Me." But now it has a double entendre, which is kind of a metaphor for my life.

—TEDDY BRECEDA

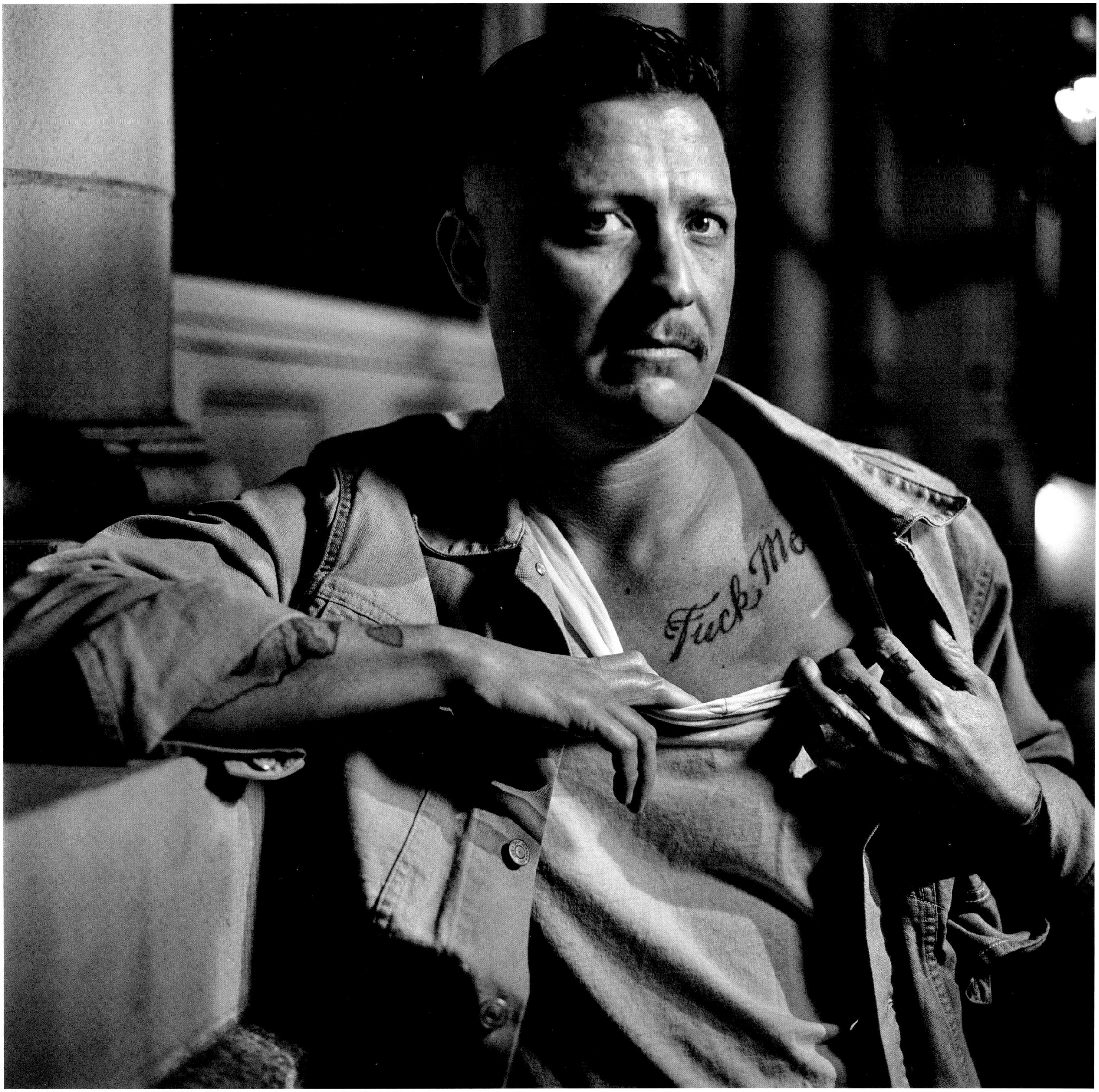

TEDDY BRECEDA

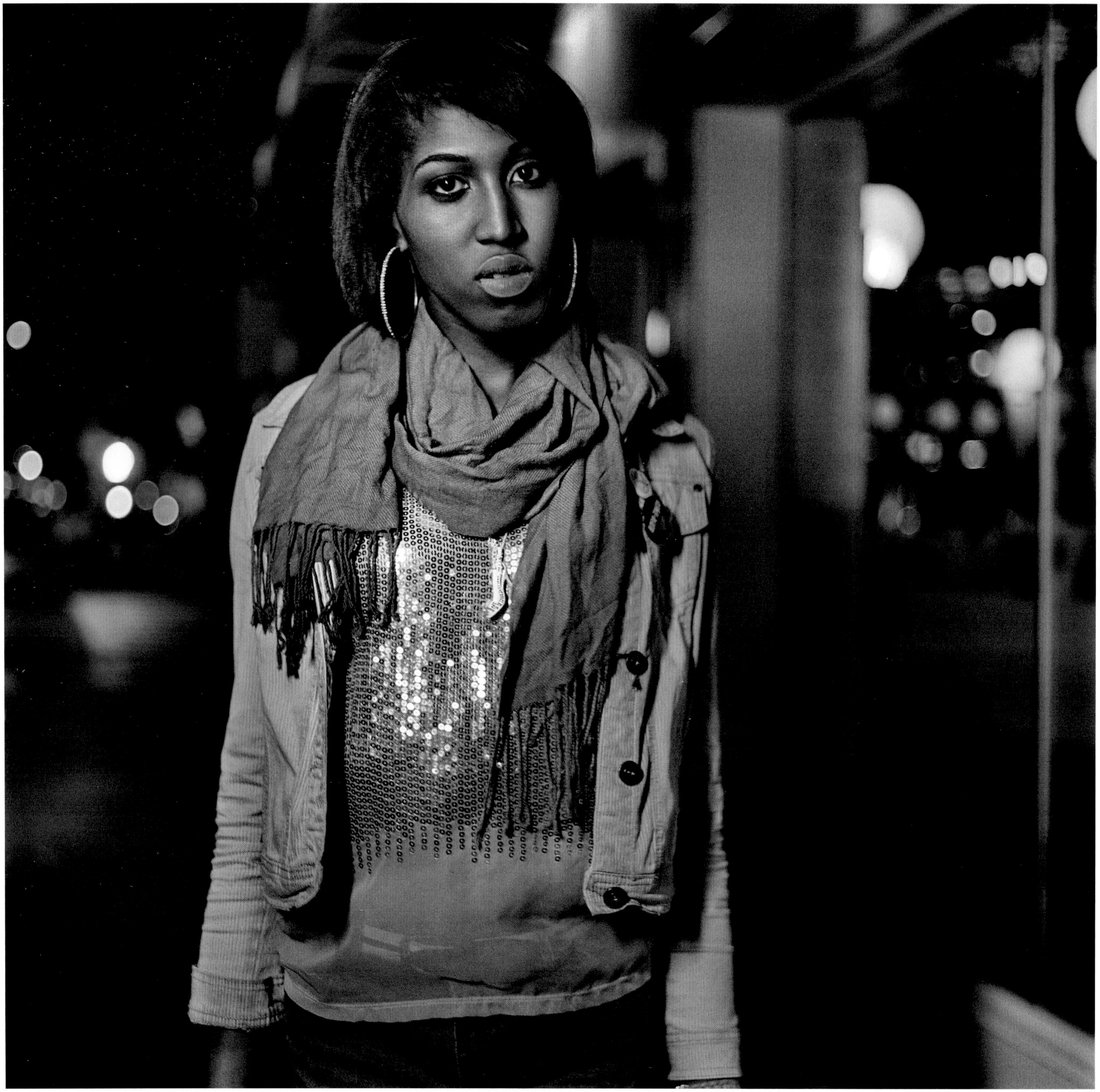

ALANI HOUSTON

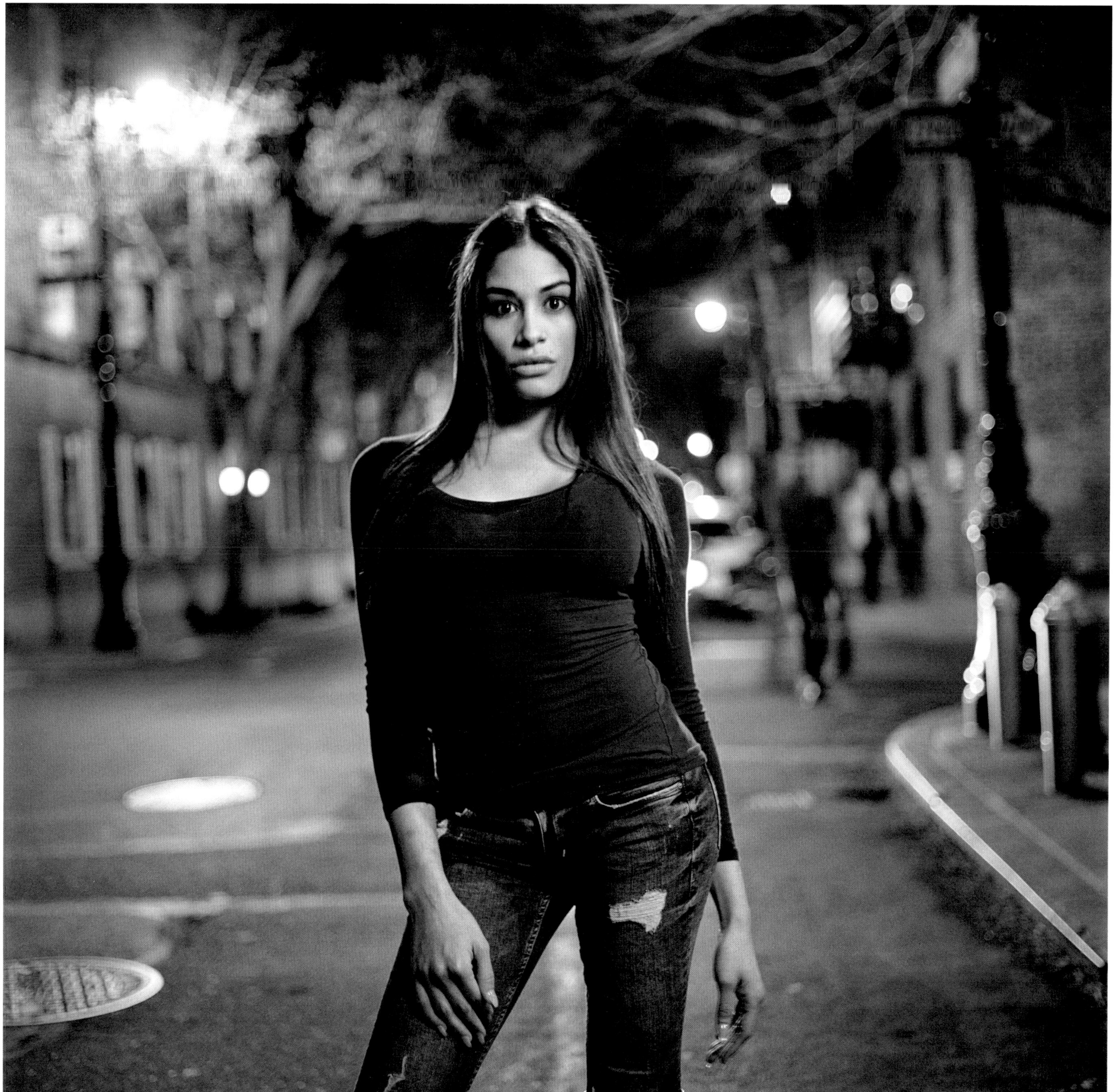

"I was a good old stone butch. But even then, I knew I wanted to be a man. I knew I was in the wrong body; I struggled to do that for twenty-one years. I couldn't wait to get the first shot of testosterone into my veins. When I had top surgery, I woke up and I was the happiest man alive."

— LESTER COOK

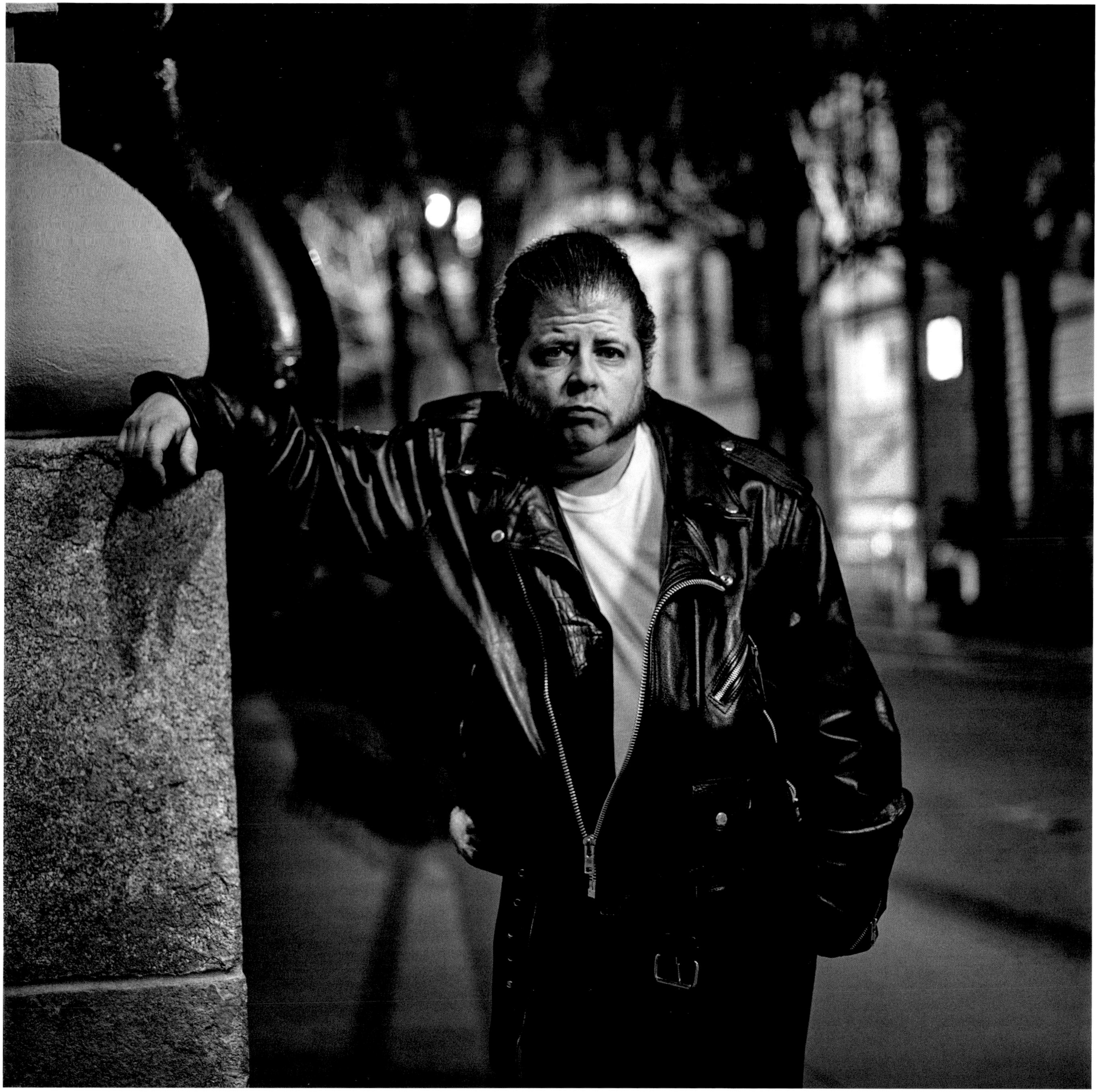

LESTER COOK

I STARTED TRANSITIONING at sixteen years old, but I knew I was born in the wrong gender since I was about two years old. When I first transitioned, it was very hard. My mom raised me on her own—I never knew my father—and she raised a son, so it was really hard on her when I transitioned. I asked her for help and she turned her back on me. We stopped talking for two years. Now we have a great relationship, but it takes time to learn and understand and be educated.

I am a recording artist and an actress and a model, and to be transgender and to be a musician, it's been a very hard road for me. The world isn't ready for it. I want to make it on the radio. I want to make it on the Billboard charts. I want to be on MTV. I want to be mainstream, I want to make an impact. Being trans, I have to work fifty times harder. And I know a lot of other trans artists can relate to this. I'm not doing it just for me; I'm doing it for the community. It's to show the world that we can be talented. To show the world, we're not all in porn, we're not all escorts. And I have nothing against people who do that—do what they have to do to survive. I've done it, too. I had to sell my body to survive, because I didn't want to be homeless. But then, you move up and you do things to better your life. I want to teach girls that, regardless of where you come from or what you've struggled with, you can be a star.

I've been very fortunate as a transgender woman. In certain situations, I've pretty much had an angel watching over me. The first time I was able to have sexual intercourse, with my new vagina, was in 2000. It was the most amazing feeling. And it was very emotional for me. But I felt kind of like I was misleading him. I didn't feel true to myself. I felt a little bit messed up because I felt like I was lying to him. I wanted to be honest, and I ended up telling him after, because he had already said he loved me.

He was a police officer. And after I told him, he pulled a gun on me. He was not happy, to say the least.

I asked him if he would still love me, if I had been born different and he started getting really, really upset, but I continued. I asked him, "If I was born a boy but now I'm a woman, would you still love me?"

He started getting psycho: his eyes were twitching and his face was red, full of embarrassment and craziness, and he pulled—literally—pulled out his gun from the top drawer of his closet. He was like bona fide, legit, losing his mind.

And I had to lie myself out of that one. I was just like, "You know I'm playing with you, right?"

And ever since then, never again. I never lied about who I was.

Every time I get serious with a guy, I say, right off the bat, before sex: "I'm trans."

—Nikki Exotica

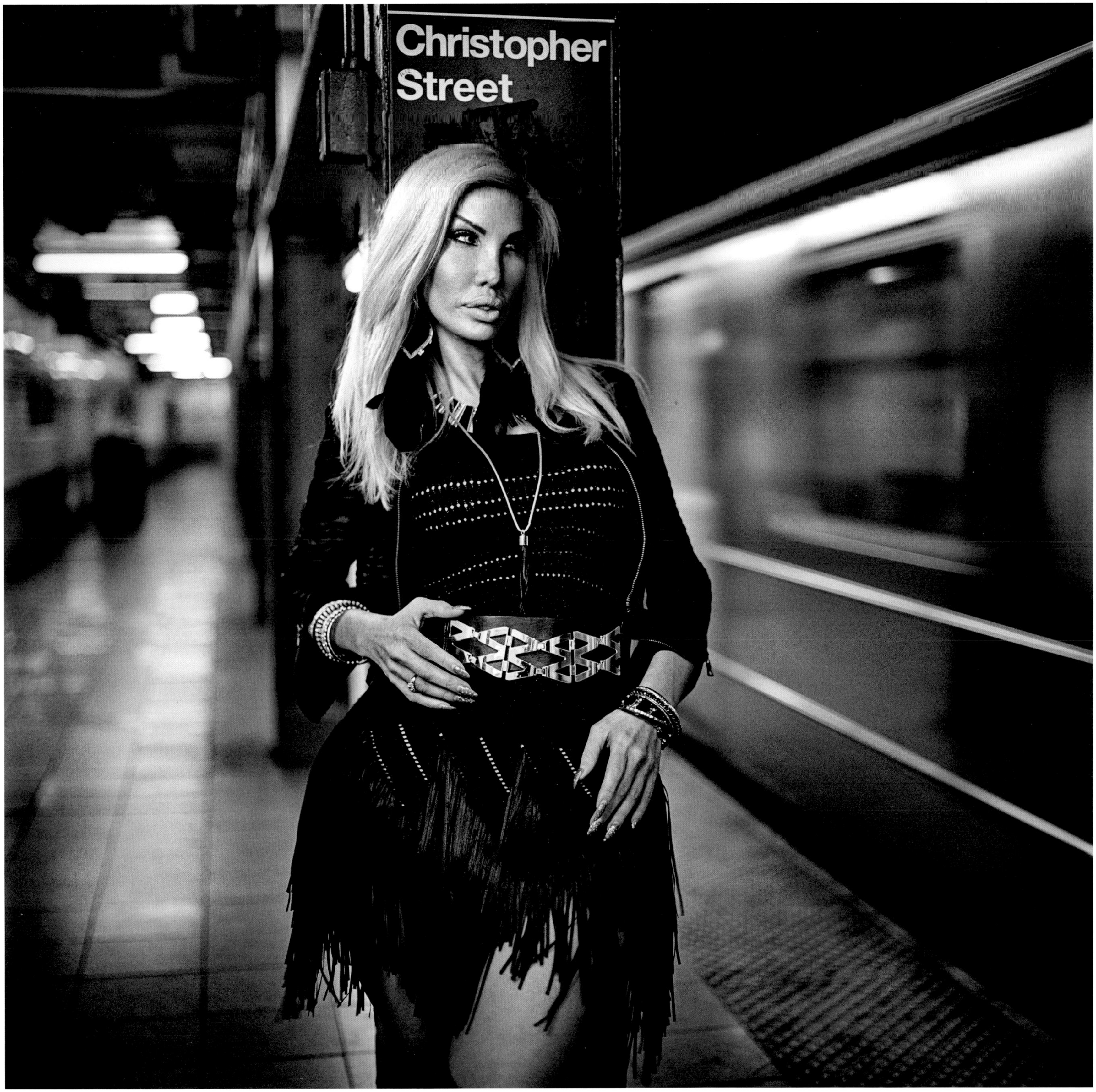
Christopher
Street

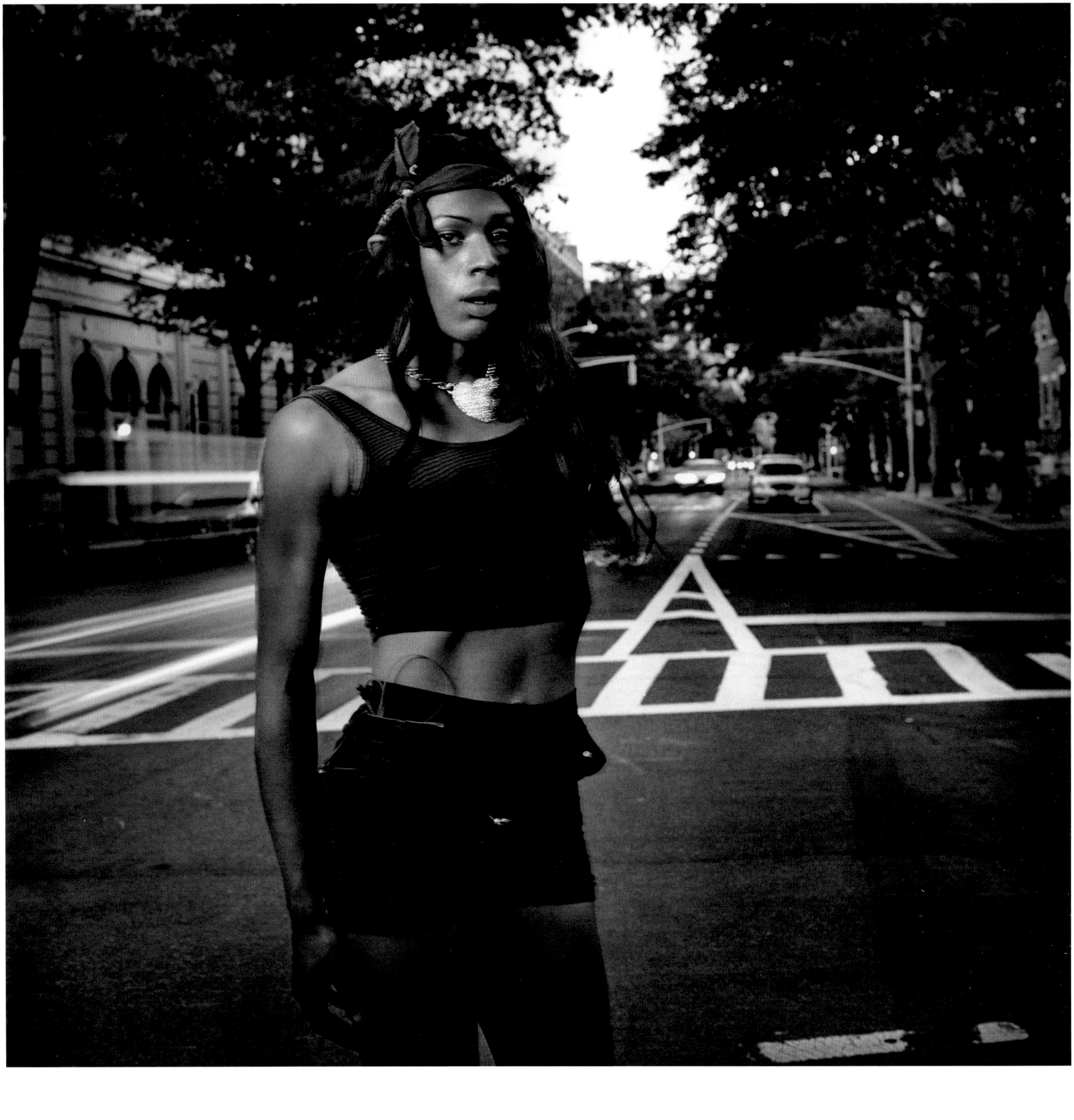

SEQUOIA HONEYCUTT

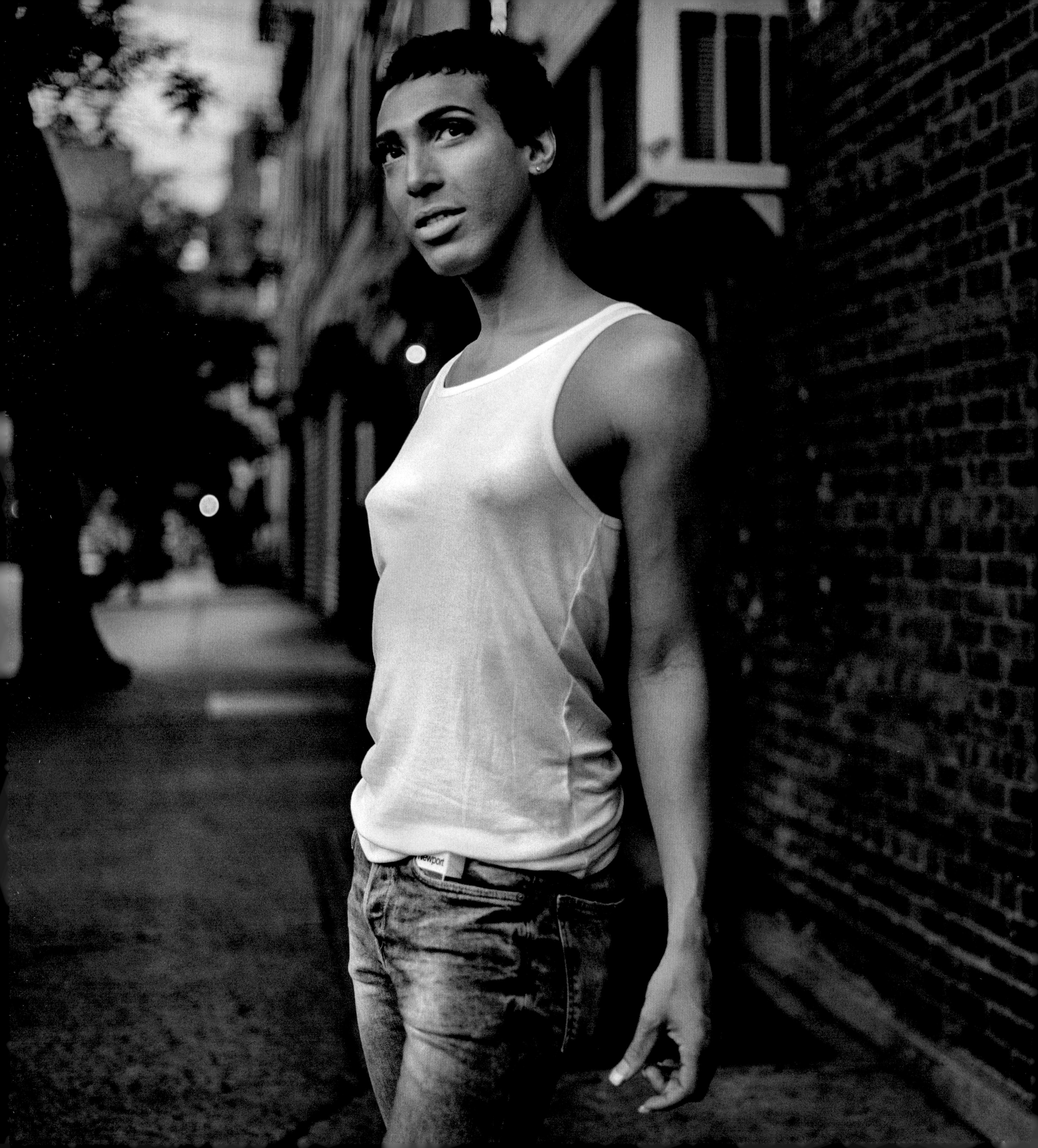
Newport

"I encourage everyone to be creative with their transition and allow it to show you where it's coming from. Stay out of trouble, focus on you; don't focus only on your appearance. Focus on your mind and your emotions, be healthy, be sane, and just be as happy as you can be. I know that a lot of people aren't happy every day, but at least try to put a smile on your face before you leave your house. And when you leave your house, if you see someone looking at you, smile at them, because they might smile back."

—MONA KIS

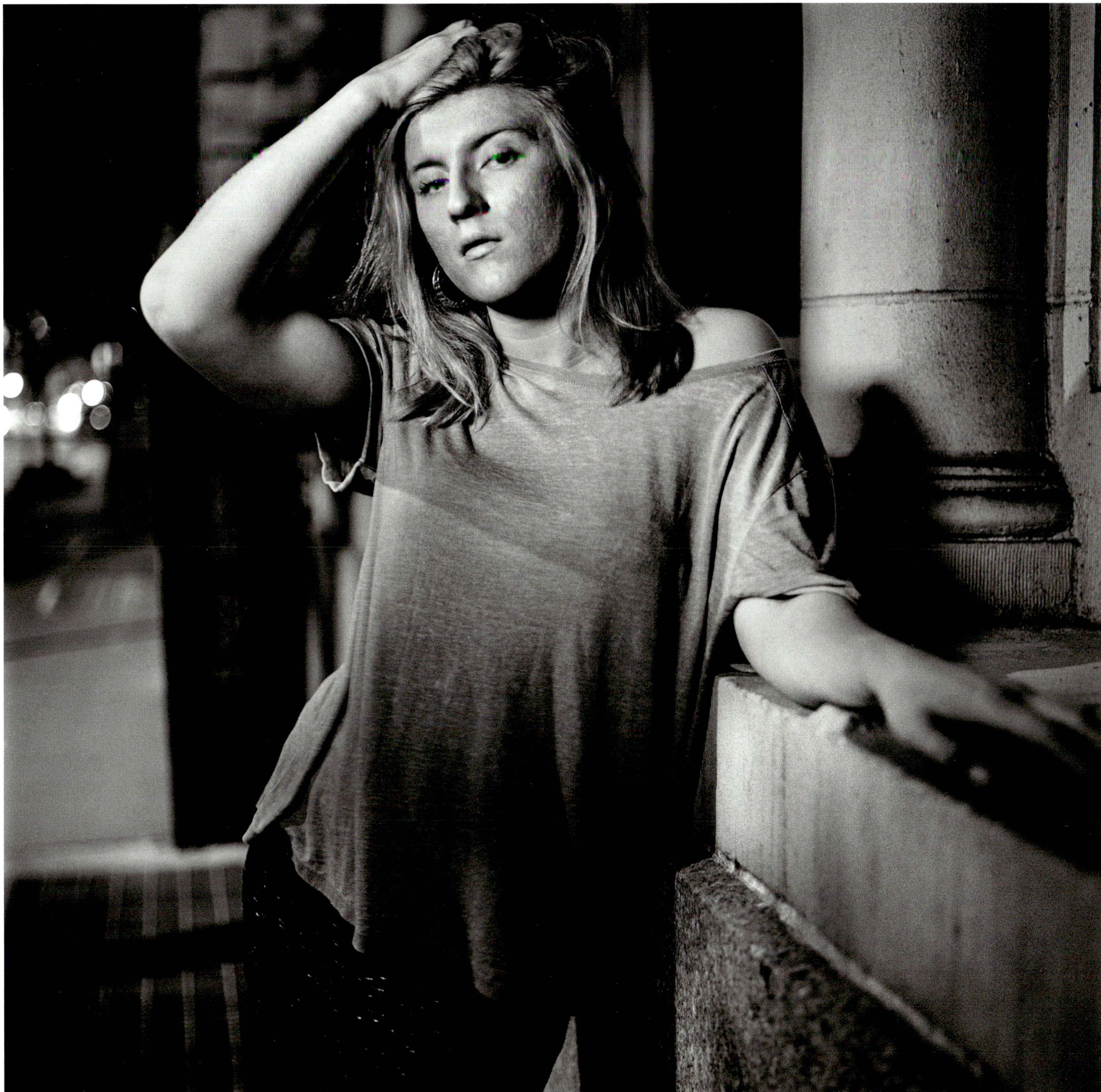

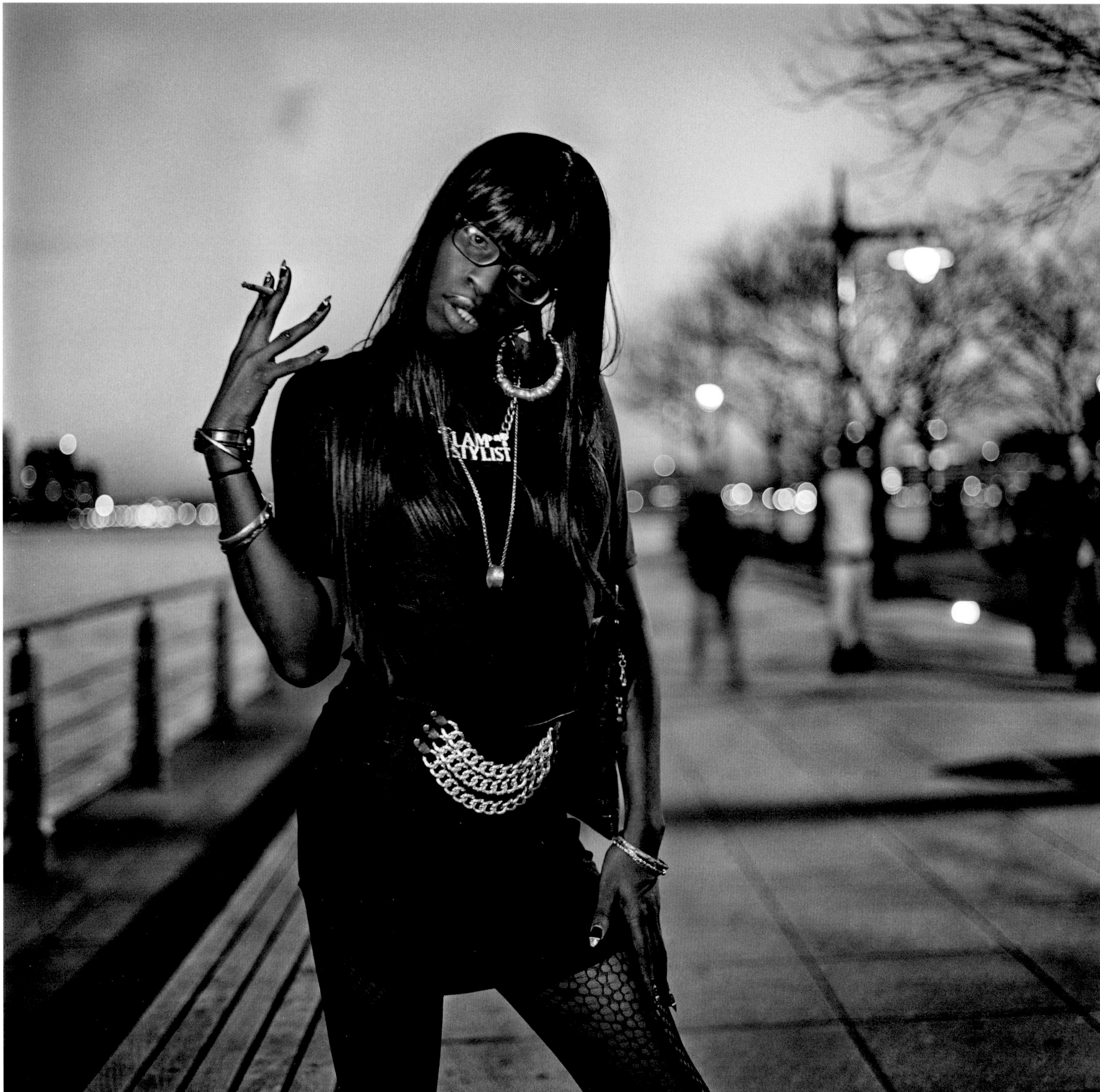

VICKYANA TORRES

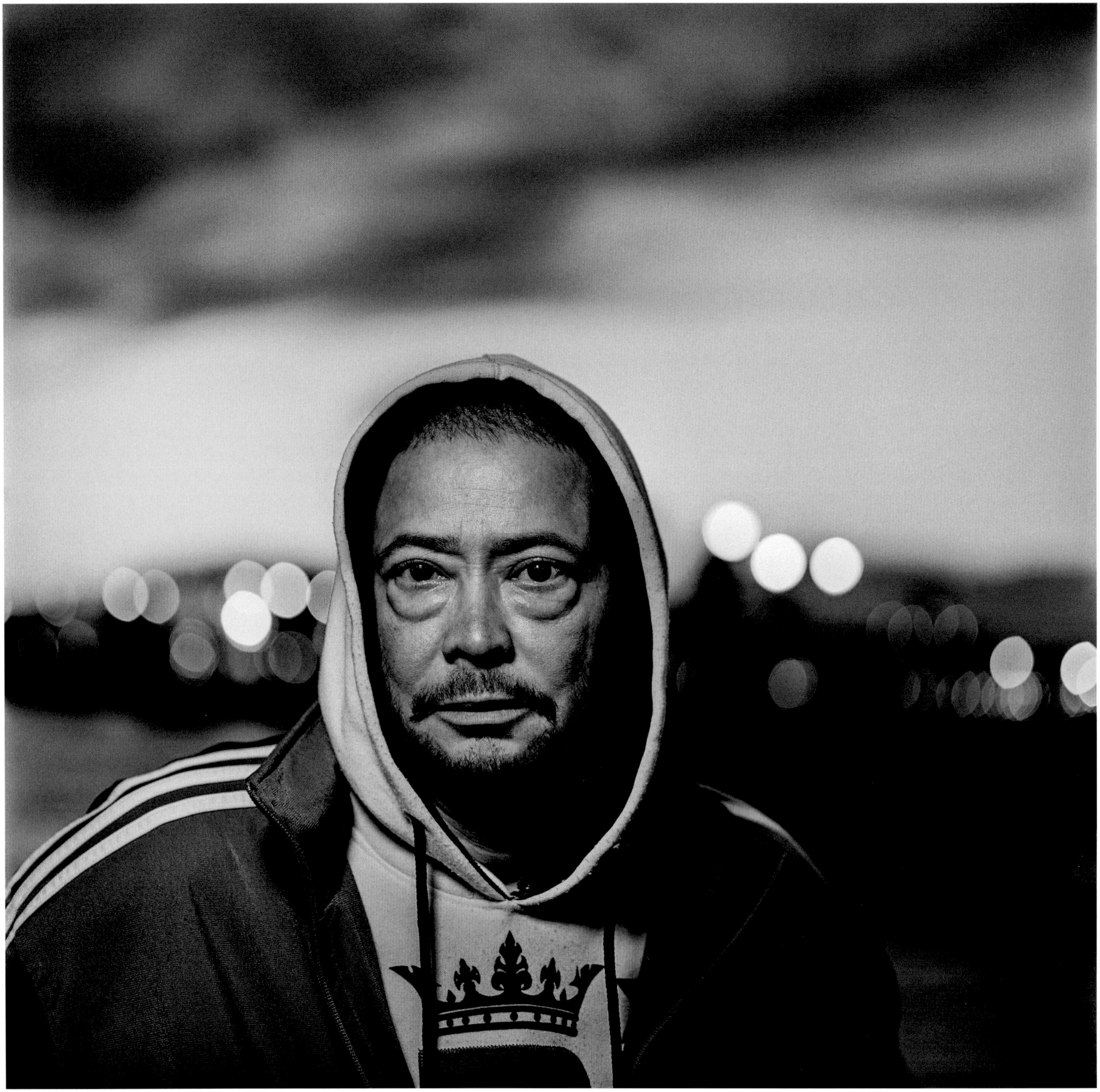

SUKIE HERNANDEZ

"The advice I would give is like the advice I took: surround yourself with people who give you support."

SUKIE HERNANDEZ

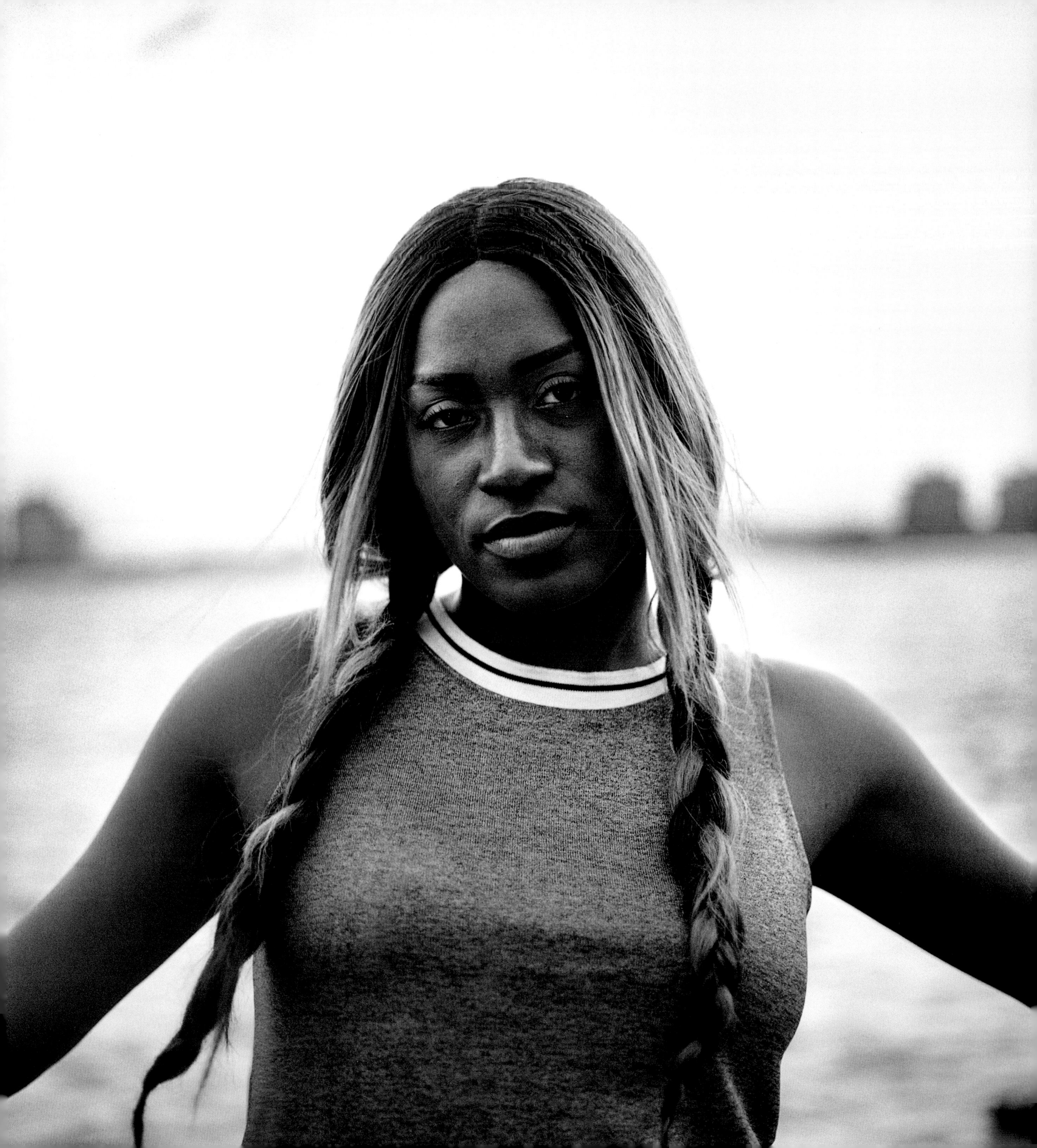

WHAT MADE ME want to transition was when my great-grandmother passed away and I became homeless and had nothing to do. I was on a lot of drugs and just wanted to transition quickly. I came down to Christopher Street and I felt like it was going to be fun, like life was going to be a party. I decided I wanted to be like all the young people, living freely. Christopher Street was like a big gay world for me.

Seeing other transgender women on Christopher Street was very inspiring for me and helped me with my transition.

When I was little, I wanted to look like Lil' Kim, but I knew I couldn't because I wasn't born a girl. I showed my doctor three pictures of Lil' Kim, and I feel like I'm the closest they got to her. I went to a doctor in Mexico without any passport, without any ID. I don't even know how I got out there. I just wanted to make my dream come true.

But there is a dark side to Christopher Street—a lot of drugs and prostitution and a lot of people without homes or families. And a whole lot of crystal meth. Ecstasy. Molly. And it's causing people to die from drugs or overdose, and it's causing HIV. Christopher Street is a very dark place. It's become better, but there's still a lot of kids out there prostituting and doing drugs. Doing drugs when you're transgender can be fatal. You're on hormones, and you're really not supposed to do all that.

When you come to Christopher Street, you have to be careful who tells you what and who gives you what kind of information, because not everybody's information is good.

The first time I had sex, I was nine years old. I was fully gay. I had a cousin who was the same age as me, and we started sleeping together. He wanted to be the father and wanted me to feel like a mother. So I got into being feminine and gay when I was very young, and I really had no chance of being anything else.

—Jamila Pratt

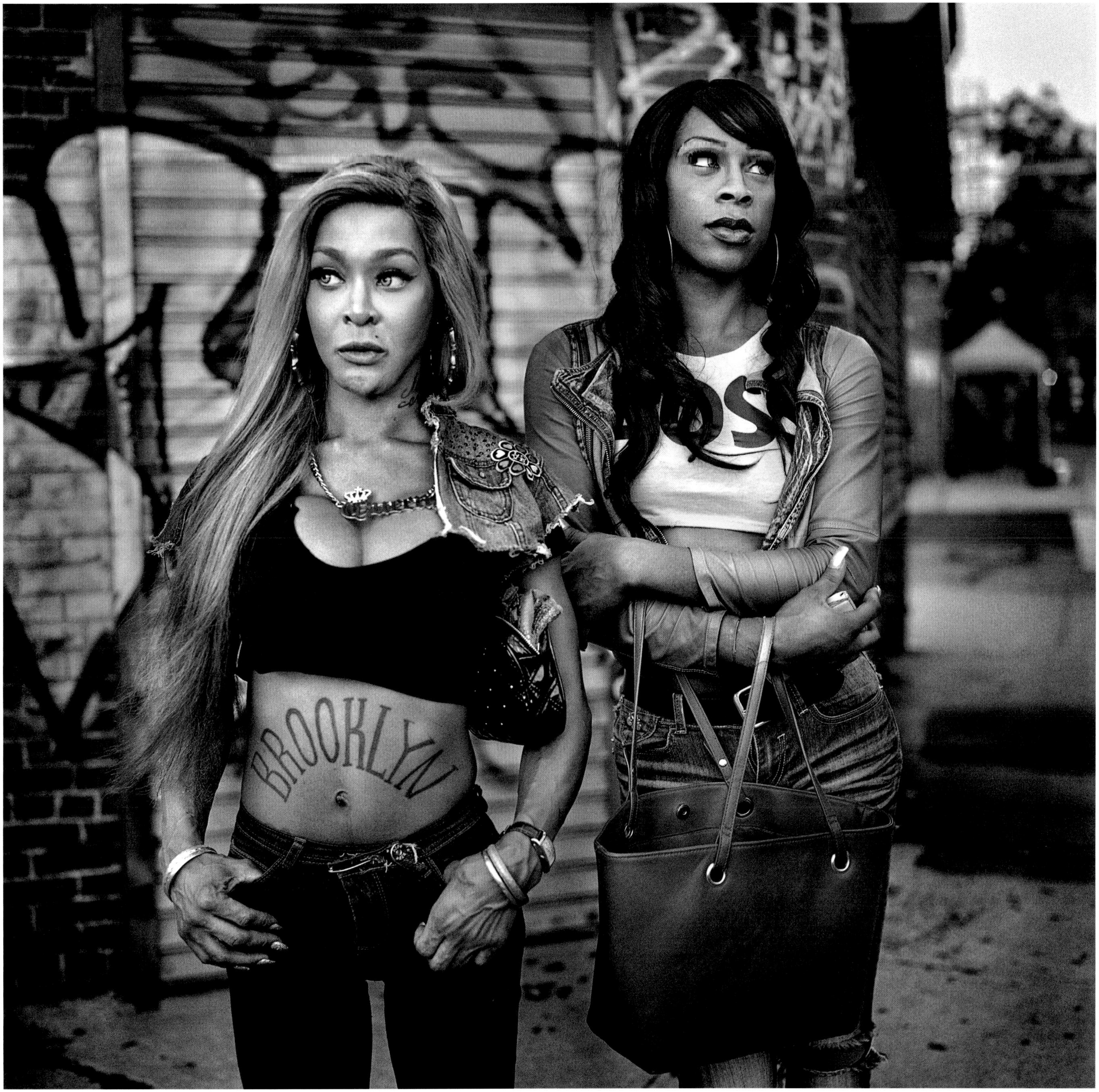

JAMILA PRATT AND PARIDISE VALENTINO

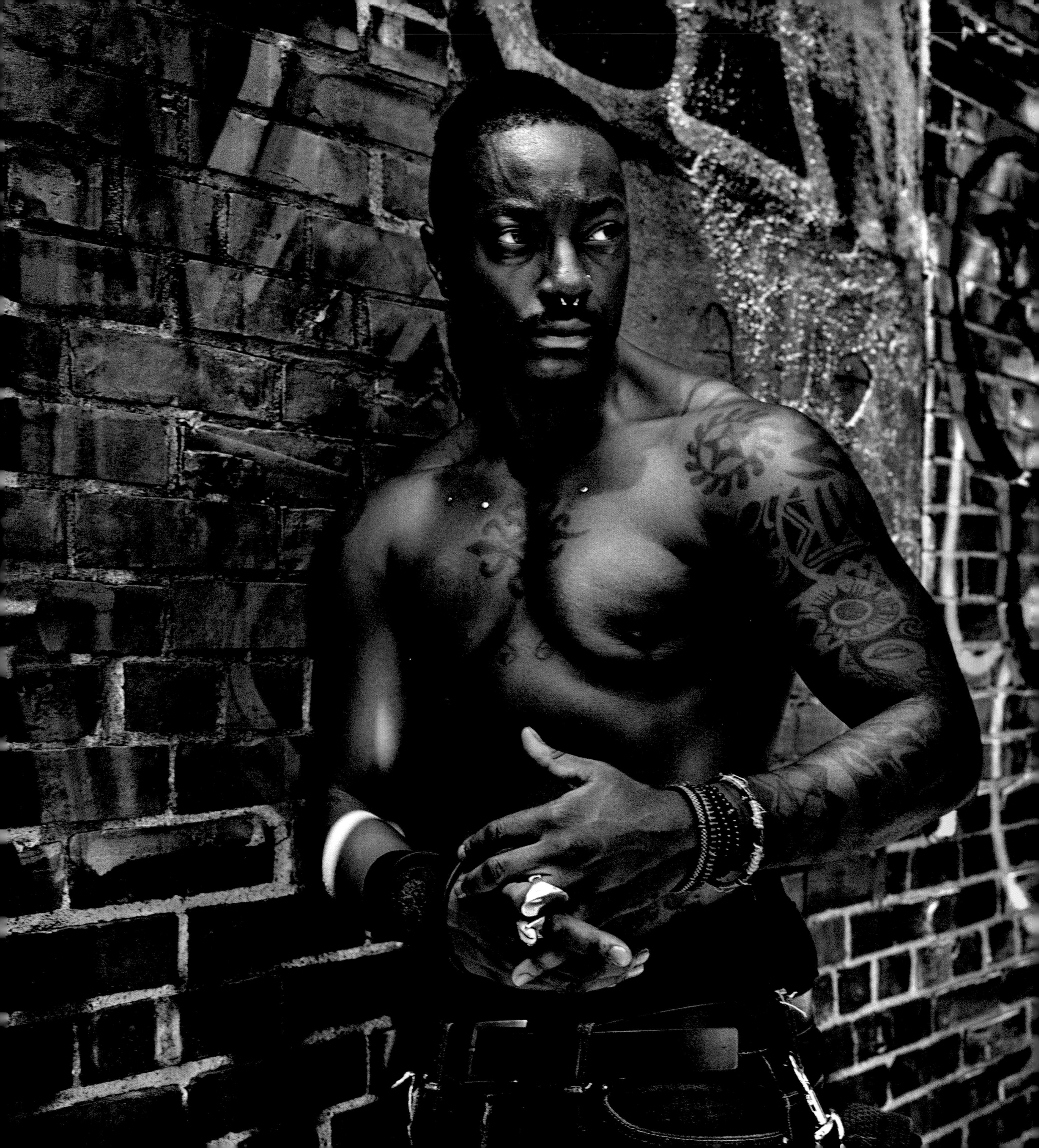

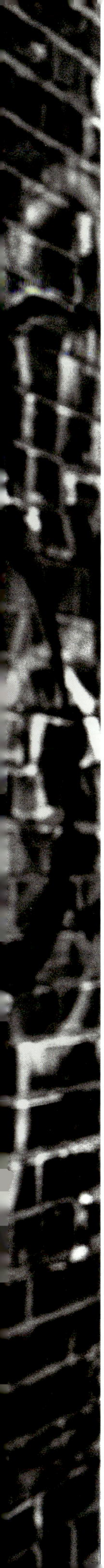

"The danger of being trans and telling people is that they tell other people. I don't think they realize they are putting you in physical danger."

—NI'TEE SPADY

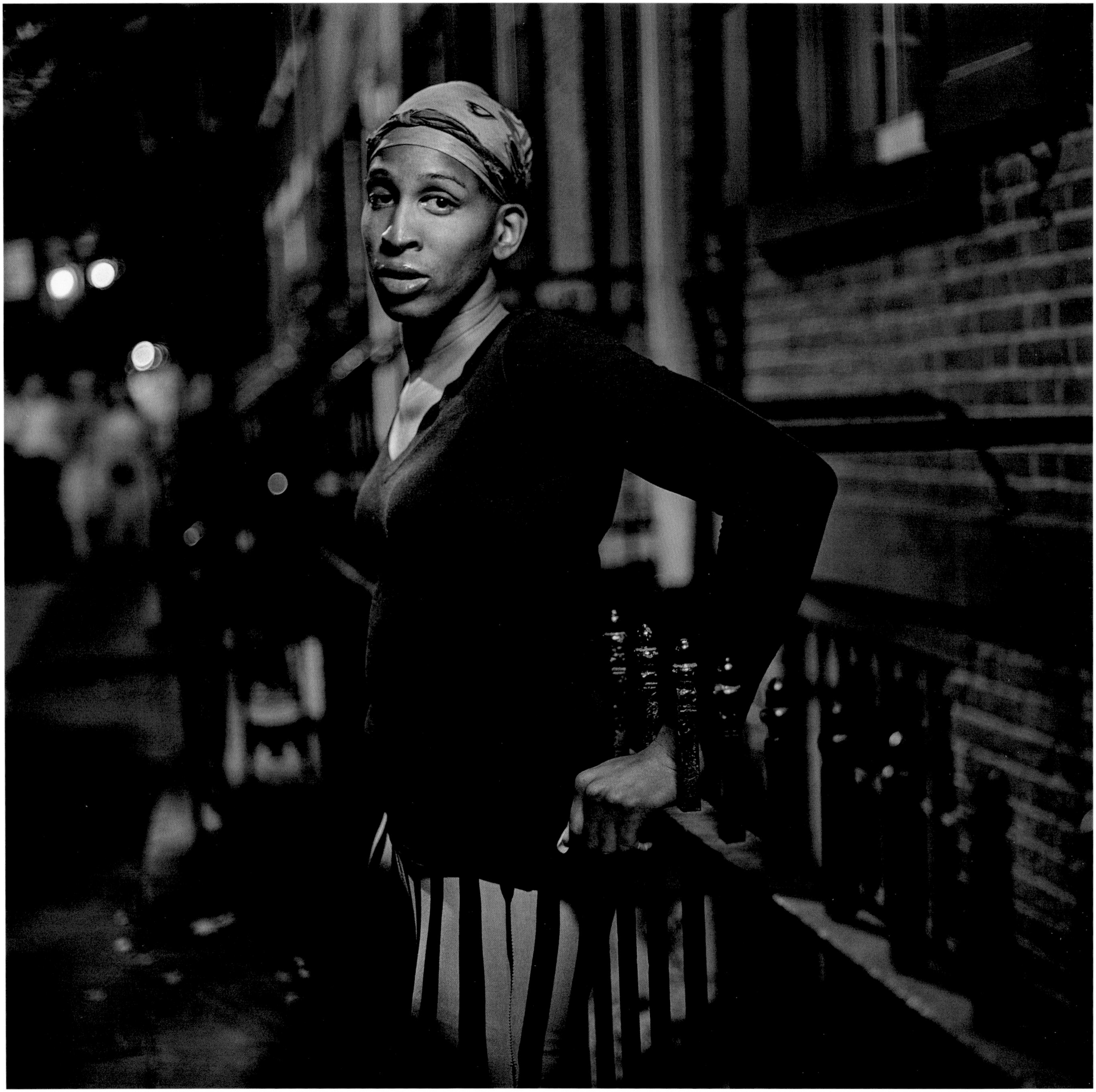

JAMILLHA LIVINGSTON

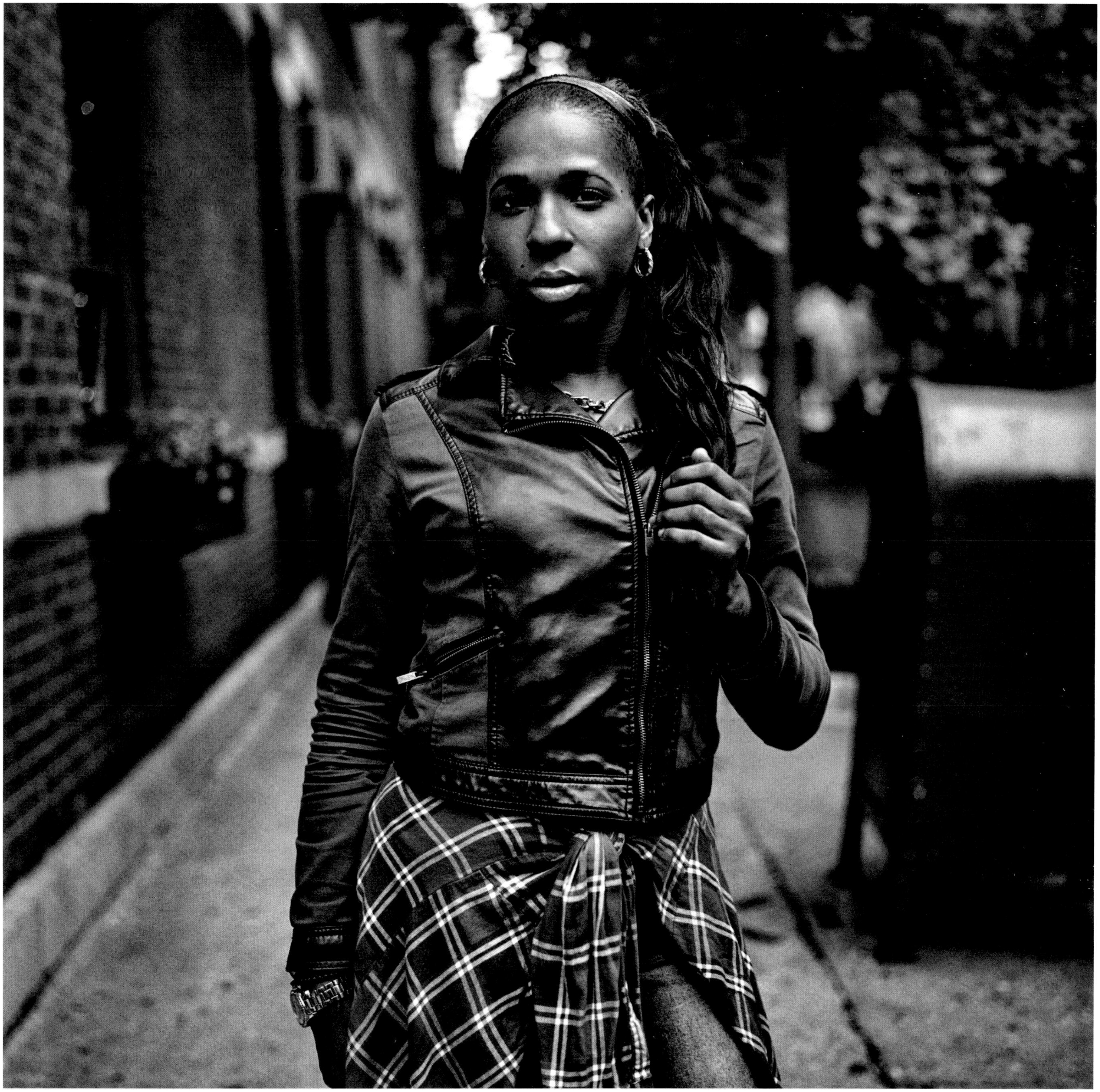

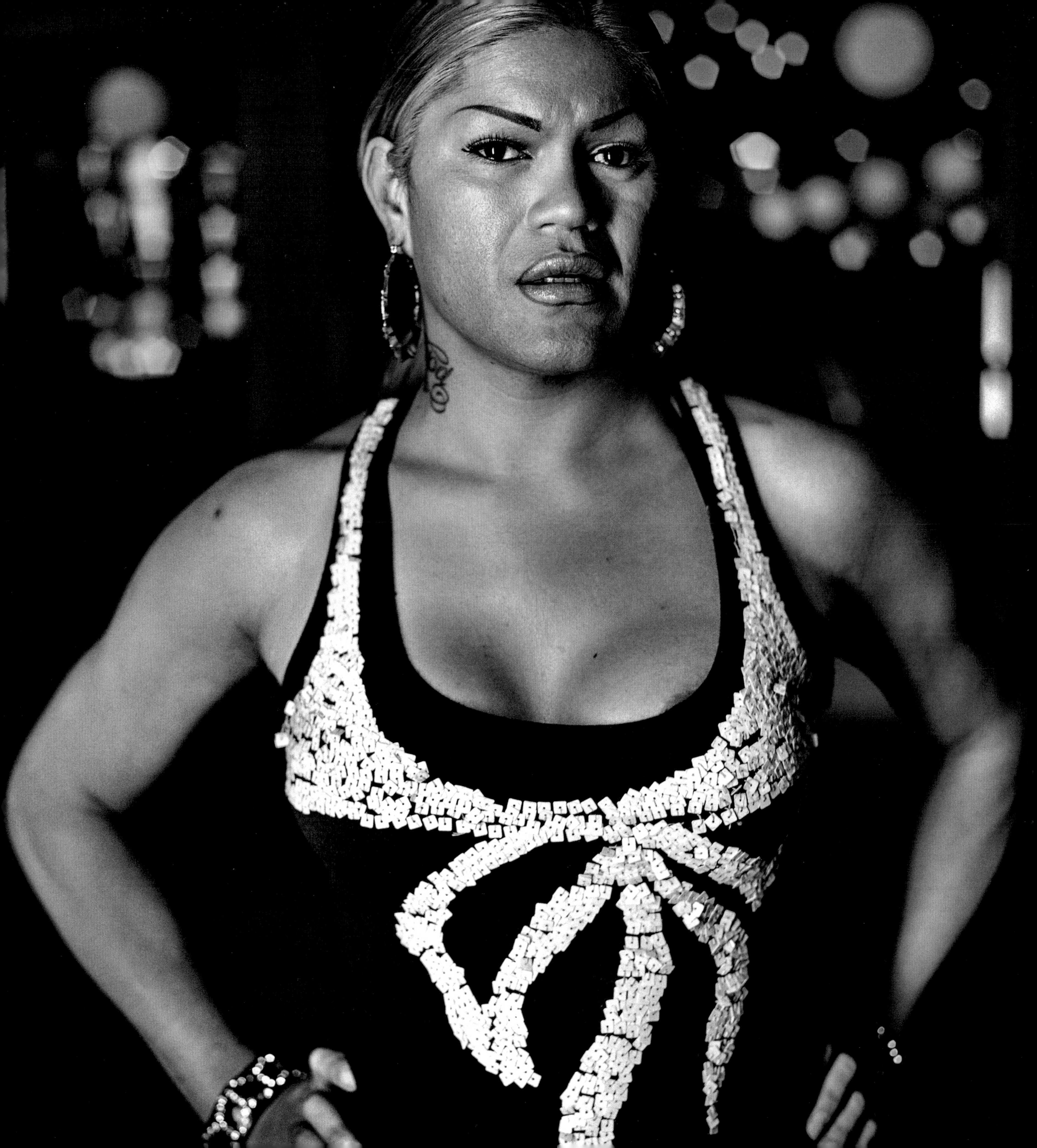

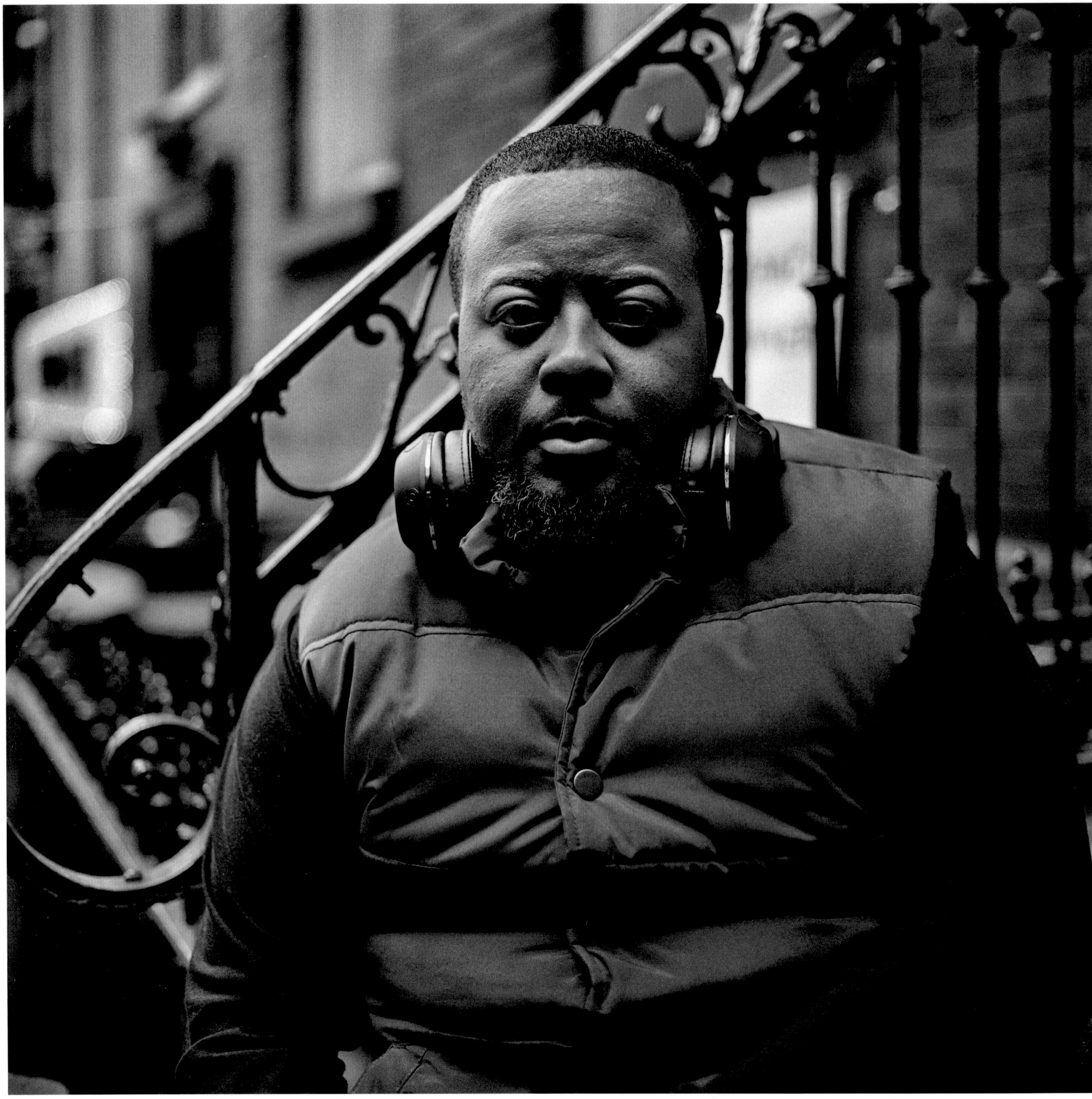

KAYDEN COLEMAN

IT WASN'T A DECISION. I had top surgery and in order to have top surgery I had to be off of Testosterone for six weeks prior to. Apparently in April, 2013, I got pregnant but I didn't actually know until September of 2013. So when I found out, I was already five and a half months pregnant. At first we were in total shock and then we just jumped into action.

The staff at the hospital was nice enough—I'm sure their intentions were good—but it was horrible and traumatizing. They didn't know how to handle me so they handled me like a woman. There was a line of people who kept coming in and out of my room like I was like a circus monkey.

I requested a C-Section and they were fighting me on it and were really adamant about having a natural birth and finally I was like, I'm done and I had a nervous breakdown. I was like, you guys are going to cut this baby out of me and that's what happened.

And she's amazing. As far as being a trans parent, maybe that will be a thing when she's older, but right now, we're just parents.

— Kayden Coleman

"I went over to my grandmother's house one day at lunch, sat down with her at the table, and played a game of Scrabble, and I said, 'Grandma, I have something I need to tell you.' I told her that I was trans, and that I wanted to be a girl. She just looked up at me, in the eyes, and said: 'Then I know one day soon I'm going to have a very beautiful granddaughter.' That was all she said. And then she got up to use the bathroom. And I sat there and cried and cried. Then she came back and we had lunch."

— MIA MIKOWICZ

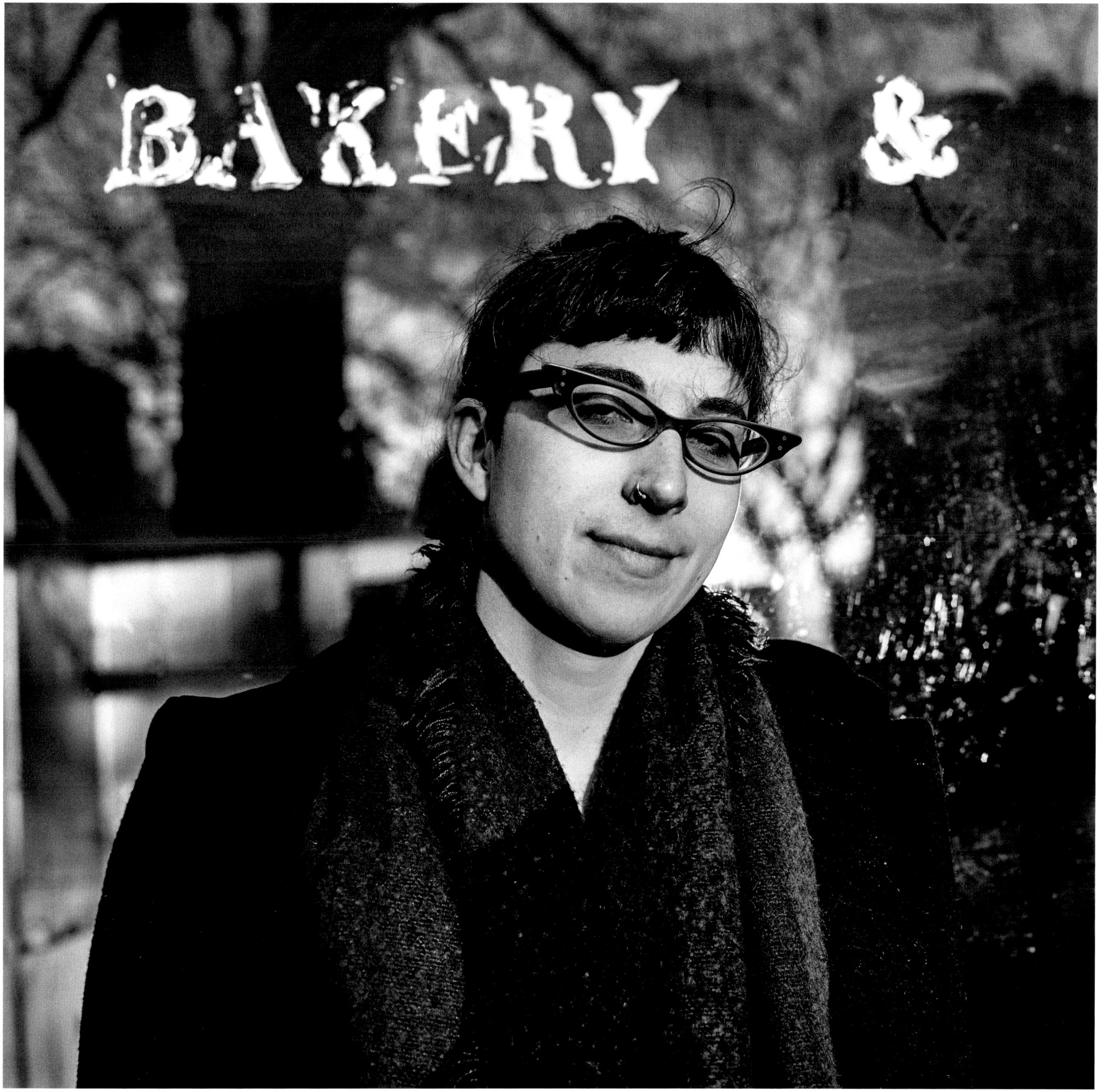
BAKERY &

"People think that because they see you changing so much on the outside, you must be changing on the inside also. But really what it feels like is that you're standing still, and slowly you're bringing your authentic self towards you. I don't think I can overstate the term 'living authentically,' because that's what it finally feels like."

—DANA LEVINSON

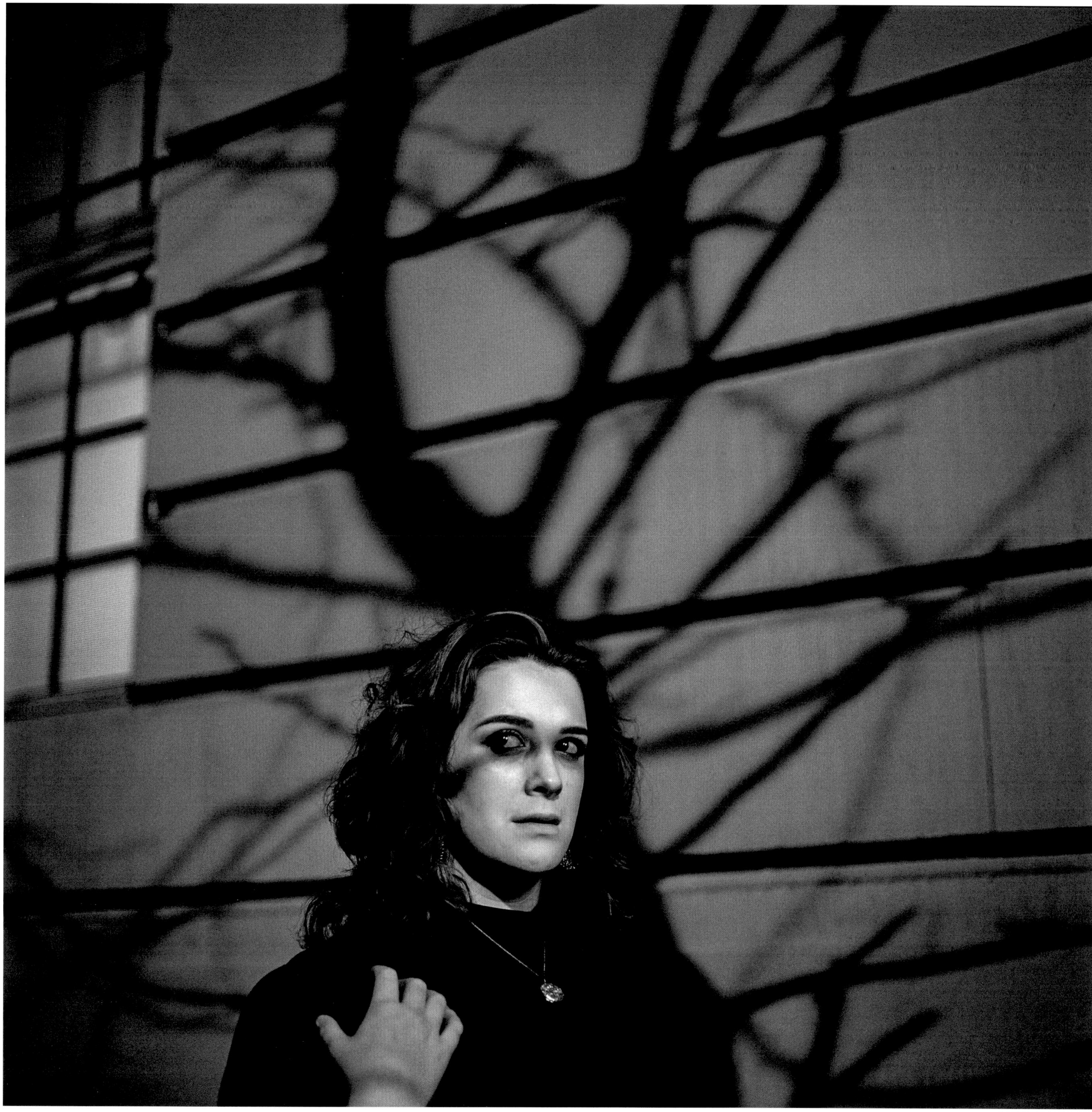

"I was convinced that one day I was going to wake up and magically become a girl. Obviously that didn't happen and I ended up having a total breakdown. I realized I had no choice—I either needed to transition and live authentically or I was going to get myself into an early grave—literally."

— DANA LEVINSON

I WAS BORN IN VIETNAM and adopted there during the Vietnam War, but I've been in New York for twenty-five years and it's my home now. I love it and I'm a New Yorker.

I was probably six years old the first time I ever thought about being a woman. I put my mom's shoes on and it just felt natural. I was a drag queen when I first started thinking about transitioning, and I realized that drag is fun but that this was a lot more than I thought it was. Becoming a girl was the best decision I ever made in my life because it was what I'm supposed to be. Most people don't understand that.

One thing that has always bothered me is when people are like, "You're passable." I always say, "Passable as what?" Guys will have sex with you, but only on the DL. It's like, no, that's not cool. Stop acting like I'm supposed to be hidden. It's offensive and rude and stupid. I can't stand the way we get treated.

I wanted to be Mother Teresa wrapped into Madonna wrapped into Oprah. I wanted to have feminine strength and be someone you could look up to, be someone who was caring and loving. I wanted to become the best version of myself.

When I was growing up, in the early '90s, we weren't exactly accepted. In fact, we were looked down upon; even within gay culture, we were like freaks. We didn't fit in anywhere, and most people don't understand that. We were like the underbelly of gay culture—the lowest rung on the ladder.

Everyone is different when it comes to transitioning. Some girls want to keep their bottom parts; other girls, like myself, go the full process. It's all personal. And it's okay if the girls keep their bits, because they are still women. It's all how you feel inside.

I was so blessed when I was younger, I worked with Annie Leibovitz and Ellen von Unwerth. But one of the greatest moments of my life was when Mario Testino flew me to Paris. It's one of those things that, as transgender, you think will never happen to you, that that industry is completely out of your world. It was beyond a fairy tale. I was in the trailer waiting, dressed head to toe in Gucci, feeling so glamorous and thinking to myself, Thank God I'm a girl. . . . It all worked out.

—Octavia McKinney

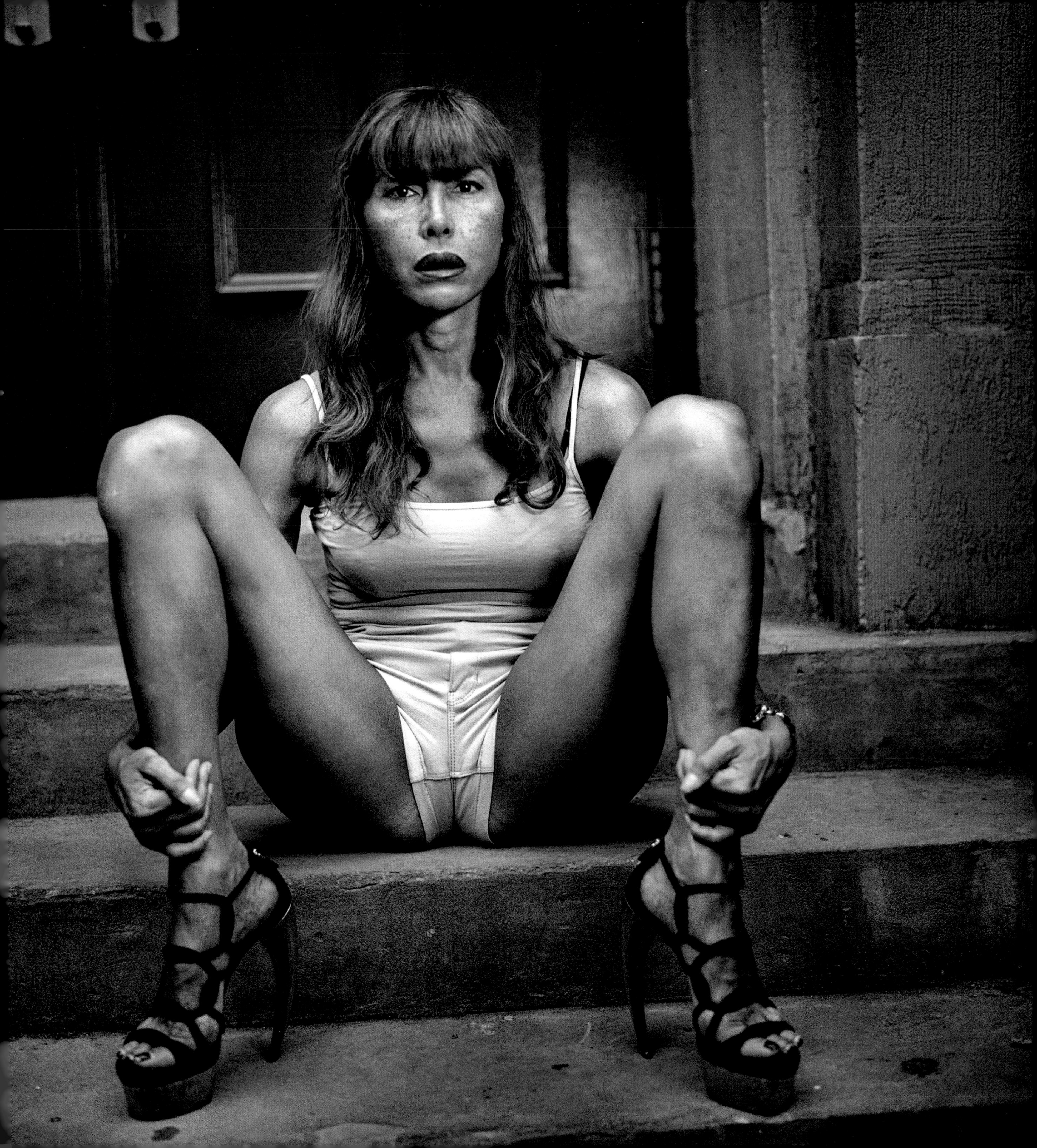

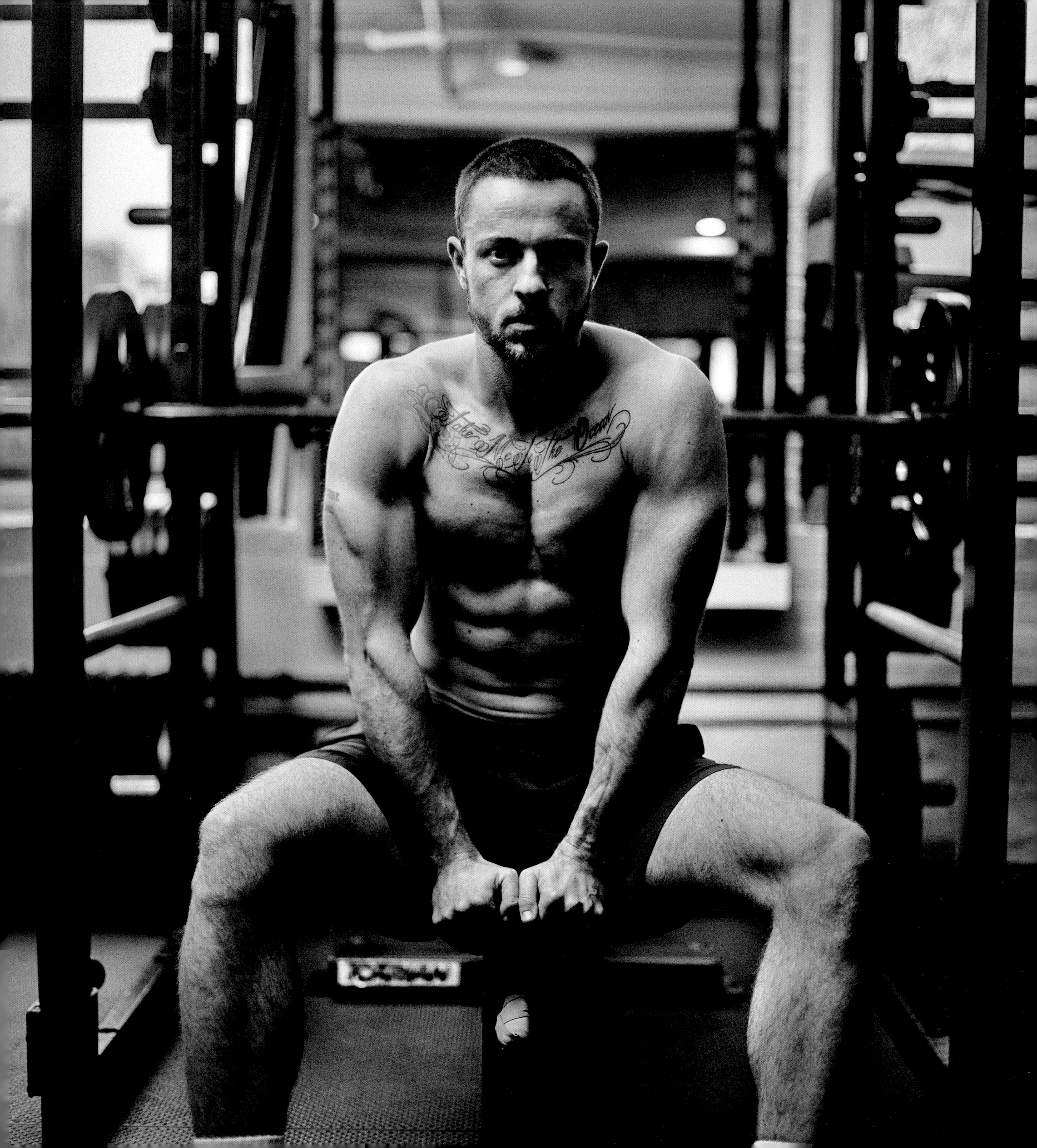

"I told my parents, and for me it was like, go hard or go home. I told myself, now you do this and you don't care about what others say or think. You're going to be a good guy. You're going to look great, and you will do this."

—BENJAMIN MELZER

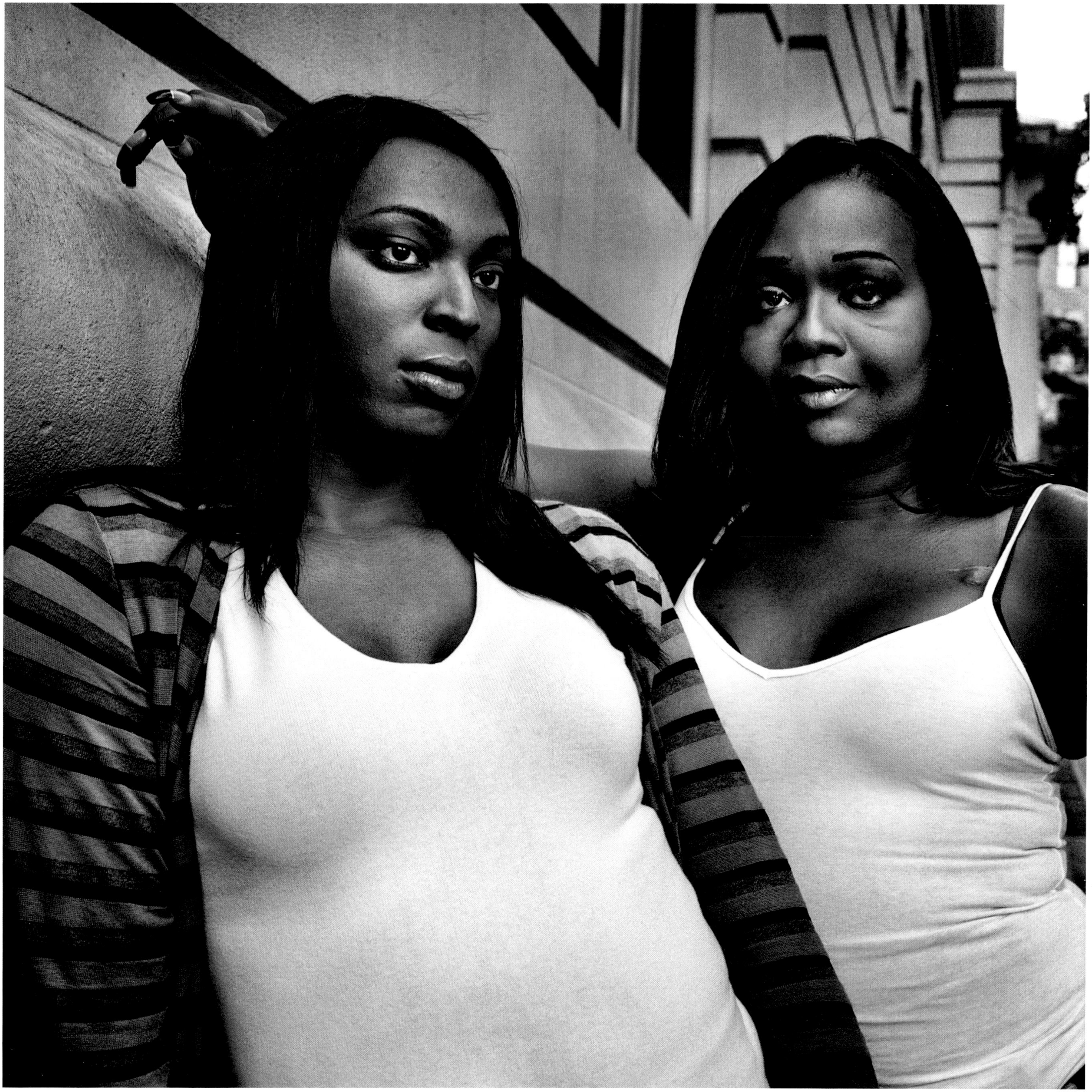

ANA WILLIS AND JENNIFER LOVE

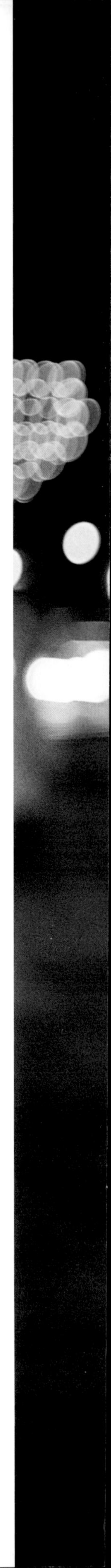

"I never saw myself as gay. I always considered myself to be just a normal girl. When I first watched 'Cinderella,' I cried because I was like, that's me."

— NISA DUPREE

IN KINDERGARTEN, I was in Catholic school in Paterson, New Jersey, and I had a crush on a boy named Anthony. I wanted to give him a kiss and I told this to my friend; judging by her reaction, I knew I wasn't supposed to like boys and that there was something different about me. Next thing I remember, I was in a parent-teacher meeting, and then, the next semester, I was in public school. I put the pieces together and realized that there were things I needed to keep to myself. I was always attracted to feminine things, and I was really confused growing up when religion came into play—like God says this and God says that and God makes little boys and God makes little girls—and I knew inside that everything I was being told was the opposite of what I felt.

In my twenties, there was this explosion of rebellion where I had to express myself, and that's one of the reasons I came out to Christopher Street. Before social media, just at the beginning of the internet, for nightlife and gay clubs for anyone who was questioning their gender identity or sexual orientation . . . all roads led to Christopher Street.

My husband's family is a really rough experience for me—they don't even accept him, really, for being who he is because they're so confused. I always try to come up with excuses for people who are not understanding or accepting. Like, is it their education? Is it because they haven't been exposed to this? Are they just really old-fashioned? Maybe they're intimidated or insecure? It could be a hundred different things. I try to give people the benefit of the doubt. I try to understand because I expect understanding of myself.

I'm still the same person my family raised, and they love me and respect the fact that I've made something of myself, but I have met so many people who don't have that. On the pier and on Christopher Street—I've partied with them; I've slept on their floor—but I always had a home to go to home to, and some of them didn't. I wish they had the understanding that I had, and I still relate to their struggle.

I feel passionately that my career and my work reflect that. I want to send a message that just because you feel you are not accepted, know that there are possibilities and there are so many things you can do with yourself. Just because you are not accepted or feel that no one understands you, you can still become an amazing, successful, smart, loving individual. And you can still have everything that anyone else has if you just allow yourself to believe it.

—Carmen Carrera

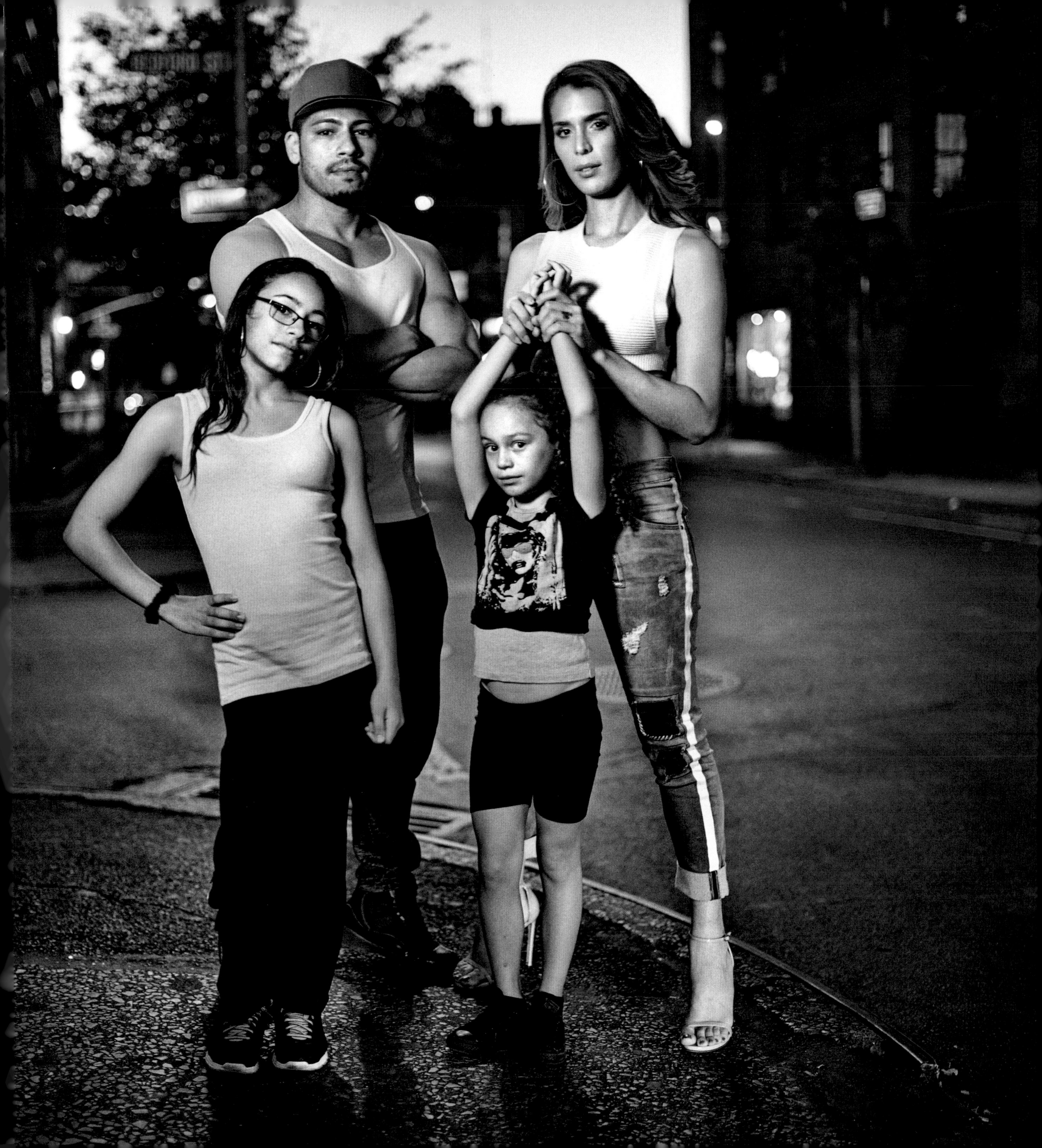

ACKNOWLEDGMENTS

To Charles Miers and Neale M. Albert for recognizing the timeliness of this project and having the interest in publishing these photographs.

To Fred Woodward and Griffin Funk for crafting such a beautiful design, especially to Fred for reminding me: don't forget to look in your own backyard.

To Sandra Klimt for her friendship and commitment to production and printing.

To Janet Mock for lending her voice with such honesty and openness.

To my staff, especially Jose Carlos Teixeira Batista, Rachel Crowe, John Kelsey, Coco Knudson, and Ruth Levy.

To Gabe Greenberg, Rocky Kenworthy, and Alex Martinengo for postproduction.

To Robert Santiago and Claudia Galindo at picturehouse + thesmalldarkroom for processing and proofing.

To Michael Hejtmanek and Perry Oosting at Hasselblad for their support on this project. All images were shot on my Hasselblad 500c/m with 80mm/f2.8 and 60mm/f3.5 lenses, using Kodak TRI-X 400 film.

To all of my amazing subjects for sharing their stories, a most extra special thank you.

To those who have contributed to this project from its inception: Victoria Anstead, Gillian Arthur, Atarah Atkinson, Alexandra Baranoff, Ryan Barone, Jakob Bokulich, Meghan Brown, Chelsea Cardinal, Lizzie Cuthbertson, John Delaney, Paris Duff, Sarah Dupont, Jenny Edmunds, Salvatore M. Fabbri, Tristan Fairchok, Maya Fell, Grant Flanagan, Adelaide Francois-Poncet, Joshua Glass, Elizabeth Gonzalez, Dante Guerra, Paris Helena, Ian Hoogenboom, Aym Icon and Transcendence Icon Company, Michelle Karch, Chelsea Lee, Erica Livoti, Anny Lutwak, Ryan Maggio, Nathan Mandurrago, Bryan Meador, Barney Miller, Jack Newton, Philip Nix, Thomas Palmer, Birgitte Philippides, Nathan Podshadley, Danielle Reuther, Caroline Rockman, Barbara Rae Schaefer, Jordie Turner, Brandon Wholihan, and Gregory Wikstrom.

A portion of the proceeds from the sale of this book will support Trans Justice at the Audre Lorde Project.

ON BEHALF OF MARK SELIGER

DESIGN
Fred Woodward and Griffin Funk

BOOK PRODUCTION
Sandra M. Klimt

TRITONE SEPARATIONS
Thomas Palmer

PHOTO PRODUCER
Frankie Mark

FOREWORD
Janet Mock

INTERVIEWS SELECTED AND EDITED BY
Periel Aschenbrand

ADDITIONAL EDITING
Lily Koppel

IN COLLABORATION WITH RIZZOLI

EDITOR
Ellen R. Cohen

PRODUCTION MANAGER
Maria Pia Gramaglia
and Rebecca Ambrose

First published in the United States of America in 2016 by Rizzoli International Publications, Inc.
300 Park Avenue South, New York, NY 10010
www.rizzoliusa.com

ISBN: 978-0-8478-5831-6
Library of Congress Control Number: 2016945009

2016 2017 2018 2019 / 10 9 8 7 6 5 4 3 2 1

Printed in Italy